A MINE OF H

by George Brailsford

Edited and Published by Jerry Vyse

ISBN 978-0-9563293-1-8

Published by Jerry Vyse (www.jerryvyse.com)
Printed by Busi-Print in Kent, England
(08452235770, busi-print@lineone.net)

ACKNOWLEDGEMENTS

George - *Thanks to Keith and Dawn Turner at the Landmark Centre for their help - Keith for his encouragement and Dawn for the many hours she must have spent putting my scrawl into a typed manuscript.*
My thanks to my granddaughter Jade Minnock who managed to do an extra bit of typing while still studying at University.
Thanks to Jane Michael for guiding me onto the next step of getting the book published.
Thanks to the Brannan family for allowing the late James Brannan's drawings to be reproduced.
Thanks to Sheila Vyse for painting the cover.
Last of all, special thanks to my wife Shirley for her patience!

Jerry - *In addition to those listed above, I would like to extend my thanks to those that helped me in the latter stages of the editing and publishing process. To name a few who have assisted: Christine Finn, Jess Neal and Patrick Acarnley.*

ABOUT THE AUTHOR

George Brailsford was born in 1932 in Mill Hill, Deal.

His family moved to the nearby Betteshanger Village five years later, and after leaving school aged 14 George went to work at the Betteshanger Colliery - first on the pit top, then down the mine when he turned 17.

Apart from a three year spell in the army for the Royal Electrical and Mechanical Engineers (and a brief period working in factories and the building trade), George was at Betteshanger Colliery until it was closed in 1989.

Now 78 years-young, this is George's first book.

ABOUT THE PUBLISHER

21 year-old Jerry Vyse was born and braised in Deal, where four generations of his family have lived.

He is the author and publisher of *Time To Go* (ISBN 9780956329301), the true story of a group of boatmen who emigrated from Deal to New Zealand 150 years ago.

CHAPTERS

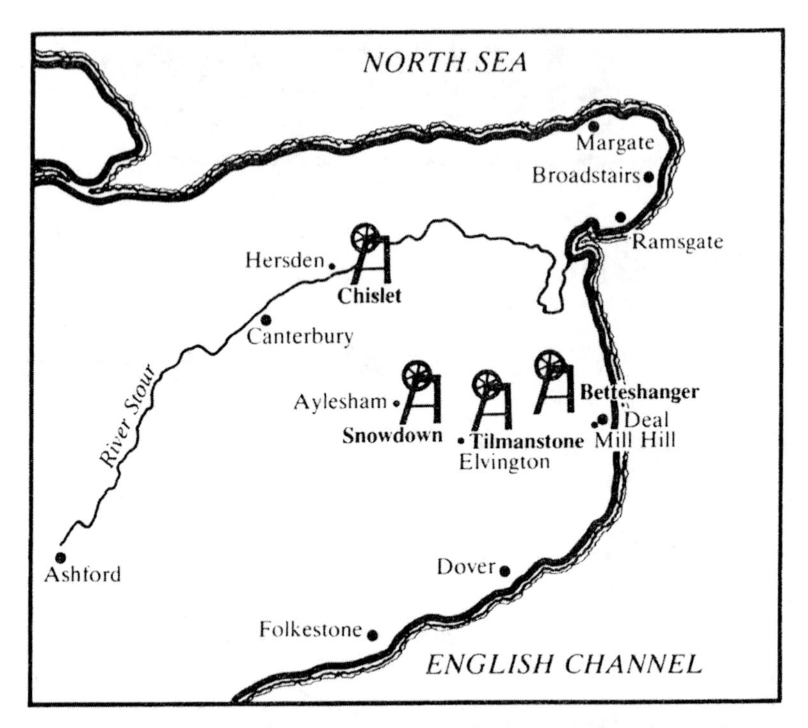

ABOVE Map showing the four main Kent collieries (courtesy of William Pitt)
BELOW Aerial photograph of Betteshanger taken in the early 1930s

INTRODUCTION

When the Kent pits opened in the 1920s hundreds of people emigrated to Deal and the surrounding areas to get jobs in the coalmines. They walked, cycled and hitchhiked from as far afield as Scotland, Wales and the north of England.

To accommodate the newly arrived miners who got jobs at the Betteshanger colliery, hundreds of houses were built in Mill Hill (Deal) and the 'Betteshanger Village'.

One thing the miners brought to East Kent was their sense of humour. It was a kind of humour that saw them through a dirty, dangerous and at times a boring job. I can remember on occasions when you thought to yourself **"What am I doing here in this God forsaken place?!"**, all hot and sweaty, or cold and wet, depending on what part of the pit you were working in.

But then somebody would come out with a 'good one' as the saying went, and you would cheer up and think of what you were going to do when you got home.

This kind of humour was also shown by their wives and families and the mining community in general, so I would like to take this opportunity to tell a few funny stories and jokes about the Kent miners, plus a few comments maybe not so funny.

Most of what I write is true, but some of the stories I cannot vouch for!

TEA

SETTLING IN AT DEAL AND BETTESHANGER

I would like to start with this story about about a family that had moved down from Yorkshire in the early nineteen thirties to Mill Hill, Deal, with the intention of getting work at Betteshanger Colliery.

The father and two sons had no trouble getting a job, being as they had worked in the mines in Yorkshire. But it was a different tale for Mary the daughter who was eighteen. Work for young girls was not easy to find in those days (there was no rubber works or Pfizers) and Mary, like a lot of other girls at the time, ended up going into service at a large house in Walmer.

One day Mary was cleaning and dusting one of the rooms under the stern eye of the lady of the house. Mary moved a settee away from the wall and looked down in disgust and said "**Dirty little bugger!**"

The lady of the house said "**Mary whatever is the matter?**"
Mary replied "**That bloody cat of yours has s**t behind the settee!**"
The lady reprimanded Mary for her down to earth language and said to her "**Another time Mary you must say the cat has left its calling card.**"

A few days later Mary was in the house on her own when there was a knock on the front door. On opening the front door Mary found the local vicar stood there.

The vicar asked Mary "**Is the lady of the house at home?**"
"**No**" said Mary "**She's gone shopping.**"
"**In that case**" said the vicar "**I will leave my calling card.**"
"**You do**" said Mary "**AND I WILL RUB YOUR BLOODY NOSE IN IT!**"

«««««««««««««»»»»»»»»»»»»»»

Lanc Evans was one of the many miners who walked all the way down to Betteshanger from the North of England. He came from Lancashire, and therefore had over three hundred miles to travel.

Lanc had been on the road for ten days and was tired and very hungry. He was walking through a village on the outskirts of London and decided to knock on someone's door and beg for something to eat. At that time it was an offence to beg and you could be arrested for vagrancy but Lanc decided to take a chance and walked up this garden path and knocked on the door. The door opened and a lady stood there and asked him what he wanted.

Lanc said **"Madam I've been on the road for ten days and haven't had a bite to eat for four days."**

Just at that moment he felt a hand on his shoulder, and looking round he saw the face of the local police sergeant. Turning back to the lady of the house he said **"And do you know what madam? I'M NOT EVEN HUNGRY!"**

««««««««««««»»»»»»»»»»»»

My Grandad B was telling us once about when he moved to Kent in the late twenties, with my gran, my dad and uncle, about another miner who splashed out and bought a pony and trap.

Grandad was one of the first miners to move into the houses that were built at the Circle by Betteshanger pit and one day he was walking to Deal when the chap with the pony and trap came along and called out **"Can I give you a lift Charlie?"**

Grandad well known for his wit said **"No thanks, I'm in a hurry."**

"BUGGER YOU CHARLIE!" said the other miner **"I'LL NOT ASK YOU ANOTHER TIME!"** and cracked the whip and trotted off before Grandad could tell him he was only joking!

««««««««««««»»»»»»»»»»»»

There was this Irish man called Tim who was one of the first men to work at Betteshanger. Tim worked on the sinking of the shafts at Betteshanger and was renowned for his strength, capacity for all kinds of alcohol and his Irish way of looking at a situation.

To give you an idea of what I mean, after a hard day working in the shaft, Tim and his mates decided to visit the Hare and Hounds pub at Northbourne. The reason for this was that Betteshanger village had not been built then and there was no Betteshanger Social Club.

After a good session in which copious quantities of ale had been consumed, they decided to make their way back to the sinkers' huts where they stayed on the pit top. On stepping out of the pub they found that a thick fog had come down. Not being local men they were not sure of their bearings, so they tried a couple of directions, but kept ending up back at the pub.

They were just about to give up and go back in the pub, when for a brief moment the fog lifted and Tim spotted the gate to the churchyard. This gave Tim an idea and pointing in that direction said **"Oi tink we should go that way, THEN IF WE GET LOST WE WILL KNOW WHERE WE ARE!"**

«««««««««««««»»»»»»»»»»»»»

The Catholic priest once saw Tim entering a pub in Deal and decided to have a little chat with him about the evils of strong drink. Once in the pub, the priest went up to Tim and said **"Tim let me buy you a drink and I will describe to you the folly of spending your hard earned money on the hard stuff."**

Tim thanked the priest for his offer and told the priest he would like a pint of Guinness.

"Why Guinness?" asked the priest **"What's the difference between Guinness and ordinary beer?"**

"Well father" replied Tim **"It's the same difference as between maiden's water and holy water!"**

«««««««««««««»»»»»»»»»»»»»

One Deal landlord made the mistake of lending Tim money when he was broke, so that he could carry on drinking. The landlord decided to put a stop to it, because Tim was still wanting to borrow before he paid back what he owed. One Monday morning the landlord was going to go to the bank with the weekends takings, and said to his wife **"If Tim comes in to borrow money, tell him he is not getting any more money until he has paid me back what he already owes me."**

Shortly after the landlord left for the bank, in came Tim with a big smile on his face.

Looking at the landlady behind the bar Tim decided to switch on the Irish charm.

"Allo me darling, it warms me old heart to see such a fine looking woman as yerself, on a lovely morning like this, and yer husband what a man, they should make him the mayor of this town and put a gold chain round

his neck with a gold medal on it and that son of yours, what a handsome young fella he's turned out to be and your daughter, she's more beautiful than all those fillum stars in Hollywood. Looking down at the dog laying in front of the fire said, that dog would win first prize at Crufts anyday."

"

Why thank you Tim" said the landlady.

Then Tim thinking he had buttered up the landlady enough came to the point of his visit.

"Could you be lending me a couple of pounds till pay day?"

"I'm sorry Tim" said the landlady **"I have strict instructions not to lend you anymore money until you pay back what you owe."**

Tim could not believe what he was hearing and felt annoyed.

"Why you old witch!" he said **"Tell your husband to stick his money up his arse and that son of yours is nothing but a great big poof, your daughter's the biggest whore in Deal and if that dog of yours doesn't get from under my feet I'll kick it in the boll**ks!"**

«««««««««««««»»»»»»»»»»»»»

Tim could not always control his drinking and now and then would be banned from certain pubs in the area. Once, he had managed to get a drink from somewhere and was on his way down Mill Road towards Deal when he thought he would try his luck at the Brickmakers Arms by Victoria Park. First of all he tried the door marked Jug and Bottle and was told by Ernie the legendary landlord to **"get"**.

Next he tried the Public Bar and Ernie said **"Tim bugger off."**

Through a befuddled haze Tim opened the Saloon Bar and with a look of astonishment on his face said to Ernie **"JAYSUS DO YOU OWN ALL THE PUBS IN THE STREET?!"**

«««««««««««««»»»»»»»»»»»»»

Tim was rarely aggressive when he had a good drink, but on one occasion when he was in the Brickmakers Arms he was making a nuisance of himself and Ernie refused to sell him any more drink. Unlike Tim's usual behaviour he said he would fight the best man in the pub. Ernie could see that something drastic would have to be done, so he said to Tim **"You see that big fellow sat over in the corner, go and challenge him."**

There was no big fellow sat in the corner, but as Tim turned to see who Ernie was talking about, Ernie took a big wooden mallet that he used for his cellar work and gave Tim an almighty wallop behind the ear with it.

Tim went out like a light and laid on the floor for about five minutes. When he came round he held his head and said **"Jaysus who hit me like that?"**

"I did" said Ernie **"AND IT WON'T BE THE FLAT OF MY HAND NEXT TIME!"**

«««««««««««««»»»»»»»»»»»»»

In the early thirties a young Derbyshire miner was making his way down to Kent to find work in the pits and after one or two lifts and a lot of foot slogging, he reached London. He decided to find some kind of work where he could earn enough money to travel by bus or by train for the last part of the journey. He was stood in Villiers Street, next to Charing Cross Railway Station and in the window of a small café there was an advert for a part time waiter or waitress.

The Derbyshire lad decided he had nothing to lose by asking if he could have the job, so he walked into the café and asked the proprietor if he could have a go.

The proprietor decided to take him on and after fitting him with a waiters' apron, explained to the young Derbyshire miner that they worked to a simple system, where every item of food and drink had a number on the menu and all he would have to do is ask what the customer wanted, check what the item number was on the menu and shout it down the hatch.

The Derbyshire miner thought this will be easy enough and waited for the first customers. He did not have to wait long. In walked two prison officers, who asked for a cup of tea each. The lad checked the menu and a cup of tea was number two on the list.

He was just about to shout it down the hatch when the door opened and four prostitutes came in and each one ordered a cup of coffee. Checking the menu, our miner-come-waiter found that coffee was number four on the list.

Like before just as he was about to shout the order down the hatch, the door opened again and a 'Hooray Henry' type walked in and called out **"I say, you there, the waiter chappie, I would like a chicken curry and be quick about it as I have a train to catch."**
This got the Derbyshire lad's back up, but he looked at the menu and found there was no mention of chicken curry or any corresponding number. The 'Hooray Henry' looked at our Derbyshire lad and said **"Chop, chop old boy!"**

Right thought the lad and walking over to the hatch shouted
"TWO TWOS FOR TWO SCREWS. FOUR FOURS FOR FOUR WHORES AND A CHICKEN CURRY FOR A PRICK IN A HURRY!"

«««««««««««««»»»»»»»»»»»»»

There was this miner who came to Kent in the thirties from Derbyshire and took lodgings in Deal with this very prim and proper landlady who obviously did not like miners, but was glad of the money.

One Saturday after work the miner, who had left the clothes he travelled back and forth to Betteshanger in outside in the backyard, saw the landlady picking up the clothes with some fire tongs. He asked her why she was using fire tongs and she replied that she did

not want to get any coal dust on her hands. This really annoyed the Derbyshire miner and he decided it was time he looked elsewhere for digs.
The following Friday after finding lodgings where the atmosphere was more friendly the miner packed his bags and went to see the landlady to tell her he was leaving. She was in the kitchen and the miner told her that he had found lodgings elsewhere. He put his hand in his pocket, took out the money he owed her which he had changed into small threepence pieces and threw them at her feet and said
"HERE, PICK THAT BLOODY LOT UP WITH YOUR FIRE TONGS!"

«««««««««««««»»»»»»»»»»»»»

Coming from different parts of Great Britain did not stop the miners in Kent from mixing with eachother. The job of mining itself brought the men together and the children once they got to know each other at school blended a lot quicker, as children usually do.

I remember this Scots lad telling me about his sister, who met a lad at a dance in Deal, whose parents had moved down from Yorkshire to work at Betteshanger. They started going out together and things got quite serious and they let their parents know that they were an item, as the saying goes these days.

The Scots girl suggested to her mother that she should invite her boyfriend and his parents for tea one Sunday. This seemed a good idea, so the invite was sent to the boyfriend and his parents.

The Scots girl then had a word with her mother about her Scottish accent and suggested that her mother should speak more slowly when talking to her boyfriend's parents, so that they would understand what she was saying. The girl's mother agreed to this because she realised how much it meant to her daughter.

When Sunday teatime arrived the boyfriend and his parents met the Scots girls mum and dad and everything went off fine except for the girls mum overdoing the posh speaking. She was trying too hard to impress the boyfriend and his parents that the Scots girl and her father cringed every time she spoke.

The girl's brother (who was telling me all this) had been playing football that afternoon and when he arrived home after tea was finished and said **"hello"** to the visitors his mum said in a very posh Scottish voice **"John I have left you some cakes and sandwiches in the kitchen. And if you want any more bread its in the 'breed tin'."**

««««««««««««»»»»»»»»»»»»

Despite the friction between the newly arrived miners and the local Deal population, it was often the source of light hearted banter rather than conflict, not least because miners and boatmen often socialised in the same pubs.

The Black Horse on the High Street was a favourite place for union meetings in the thirties. When the meetings finished, the committee would have a few drinks in the bar. Lester Magness, a well known Welsh union man who went on to become a very active local Councillor, was telling everyone who cared to listen, that in his opinion there were not any proper s**t houses in Kent before the miners came to Kent.

One of Deal's well known boatman looked him in the eye and said **"Yes, but you make up for that mate."**

««««««««««««»»»»»»»»»»»»

Two Kent miners met in Deal High Street.

"Hallo Jack" said the first miner **"How thee getting on?"**
"Awreet Cyril hows theesen?" replied Jack.
"Not bad" said Cyril **"I don't like the look of yon sky it looks as though it is going to rain."**
Jack looked up at the ominous looking clouds and asked **"Dust?"** (meaning do you?)
"NAY, THEE DAFT BUGGER" scoffed Cyril **"WATTER!"** (Water!)

«««««««««««««««»»»»»»»»»»»»»»

A miner and his wife were quite proud of their son when he passed his eleven plus and ended up at Sir Roger Manwood's Grammar School at Sandwich. After the son had been there about a year, the miner and his wife received an invitation to attend an open day at the school and decided to attend. On arriving at Manwood's they mingled with the other guests and eventually met their son's regular teacher and in the words of the boy's father asked **"How's that lad of mine getting on?"**

The teacher gave them a very good report and added **"He is a very clever boy and could go far, but it would help him quite a bit if he could lose his Northern accent."** The miner thanked the teacher and decided he would make an effort to make his son talk 'proper'.

A week later the miner was stood with his son outside the Mill Hill Post Office when the son noticed a dog stuck on a bitch on the other side of the road and drew his fathers attention to it by remarking **"Sithee fadder yon dogs f**king t'other."**

His father did no more and gave his son a hefty clout round the head, knocking him halfway across the road and shouted angrily **"WHAT HAVE I TOLD THEE ABOUT SAYING SITHEE?!"**

««««««««««««»»»»»»»»»»»»

A story that reared its ugly head every now and then was the tale that when the houses that were built at Mill Hill and the Betteshanger village the miners and their families could not make out what the bathrooms were for. According to a minority of bigoted locals, the miners had never seen a bath before and thought they were for putting their concessionary coal in.

On one occasion I was collecting some items for the Blacksmith shop from the pit head stores at Betteshanger. Two pit top workers were stood by the counter having a conversation. I could not believe what they were saying. According to them, the miners who lived in Mill Hill and Betteshanger never got married and all f**ked one another and shared the kids out at Christmas.

I remember, only being fifteen at the time, getting so angry with these two Kent men who had benefited by being employed in the mining industry that they should have such a low opinion of the hard working miners that I called them all the swear words I had learned at that age. That evening I mentioned it to my mum and dad, they told me to ignore them and put it down to their ignorance.

My mother in her latter years moved from Betteshanger down to Cowdray Square, Mill Hill, and could not have picked better neighbours, if she had tried. On one side she had Dennis and his wife, and on the other side Nunk and his wife. Both lots of neighbours made my mother feel very welcome.

Nunk's garden, back and front, always looked immaculate as did Dennis's. My two brothers and myself, if we had time, did our best to keep my mother's big back garden tidy. Often when we were down there doing a bit of gardening we would have a chat with Nunk or Dennis.

One day I was doing some mowing and realised the front garden hedge could do with clipping. I knew I would have to go back to my house to get my garden shears, when I spotted Nunk pottering about in his garden.

I called out to him **"Nunk, can I borrow your garden shears?"**
Nunk said **"Of course you can, come round and I'll get them out of the shed for thee."**

I climbed over the fence and looked through the door of Nunk's shed and Nunk took his garden shears off the wall, and handed them to me. I looked in amazement at his collection of garden tools. No kidding Nunk seemed to have every garden implement that had ever been invented, plus a seven and a fourteen pounds sledge hammer.

Nunk saw me looking at the hammers and said **"I brought them home from the pit when I had to pack up on the coalface".**

I knew there were no jobs that Nunk would need sledge hammers for in the garden, so I said **"Does the garden get so hard at times that you have to use a fourteen pound hammer on it?"**

"Cheeky bugger!" replied Nunk with a twinkle in his eye. **"Any more from thee and I'll take the shears back!"**

Every now and then when I saw Nunk in his back garden I would call out **"BREAK THEM BLOODY LUMPS UP NUNK!"**

««««««««««««»»»»»»»»»»»»

My maternal grandfather George (Dosh) Gibb and his eldest son also called George Gibb were two of the original members who started off the Betteshanger Colliery Silver Band. To get really started they needed money from different sources to acquire instruments and uniforms. One of the ideas they came up with was to go round the miners houses in Betteshanger and Mill Hill and knock on doors and ask for contributions.

One lad who was collecting did so well round Mill Hill, he decided to carry on and try his luck in Walmer. He did not have quite the luck that he had at Mill Hill, in fact none at all, but he pressed on and saw this old cottage. He opened the garden gate, walked up the path and knocked on the door.

An old lady well into her eighties opened the door and asked him what he wanted.

Our musical miner said **"Madam I am collecting for instruments and uniforms for Betteshanger Colliery Silver Band."**
"I am sorry young man I cannot make out a word you are saying" replied the old lady.
"

"I'll give it one more go" thought the young miner and tried again. He still got the same reply, so decided to call it a day. Turning round he walked back down the garden path towards the gate and the old lady called out **"Please close the gate on you way out."**

The young lad thought seeing as she is hard of hearing she will not know what I am saying, so he called back **"F**k the gate."**

Imagine his shock when the old lady called out **"F**K THE BETTESHANGER COLLIERY SILVER BAND!"**

«««««««««««««»»»»»»»»»»»»»

My Uncle Hughie used to love telling me this story about before he came down to Betteshanger, when he worked in the pits in Fife. According to him the explosives they used at one time were in crystal form and were poured into the bored holes after the detonators had been placed and were then ready to be fired.

One day after coming up the pit he and one of his workmates went to the powder magazine to collect some explosive crystals for the next day. Uncle Hughie took them home and left them in the kitchen.

The following morning he got ready for work and by mistake he picked up a two pound bag of Tate and Lyle's granulated sugar. It was not until they were going to pour what they thought were the crystals, that they realised it was sugar.

For a laugh my uncle and his mates decided to carry on using the sugar to see what would happen. They got a deputy to fire the detonators and reckoned for the next month they were picking boiled sweets and jelly babies from the walls and roof and sucking them. (And pigs might fly...).

Another story my uncle Hughie used to tell, was about another Scot called MacDonald. This story used to vary at times, depending on how he felt at the time.

Sometimes Uncle Hughie would add a bit on and other times he left a bit out, but the basis of the story went back to the Massacre of Glencoe. This was where the Campbells slaughtered the MacDonalds.

Uncle Hughie's middle name was Campbell and this MacDonald fellow was sent to work with him. Uncle Hughie decided to keep quiet about his middle name. One day, however, Mac saw my uncle's docket or payslip and read the name Hugh C Gibb.

"Hey Hughie what's the C stand for?" he asked.
Uncle Hughie refused to tell him. The MacDonald fellows face twisted into a snarl and he spat out **"You're not one of those Campbell bastards are ye?"**
"No" replied Uncle Hughie **"Nothing like that."**

MacDonald never mentioned it again until he was having a farewell drink with Uncle Hughie and some other mates. As he shook hands with Uncle Hughie he said **"I'm glad you are not one of those f**king Campbells."**

"So am I" said Uncle Hughie **"BECAUSE THEY DIDN'T DO MUCH OF A JOB AT GLENCOE. THAT'S WHY WE HAVE GOT ALL THESE BLOODY RESTAURANTS!**

«««««««««««««»»»»»»»»»»»»»

A Scottish doctor who was part of a practice in Deal had a reputation as a no nonsense medical man as most Scottish doctors seem to have.

Trying to get another week off work when you had been sick or injured was nigh on impossible, if he thought you were swinging the lead. Any miner from below the border would be told **"Get ye self back to work ye idle bugger there's not a thing wrong with ye!"**

Yet any miner from Scotland would not hear anything bad said about him and would often tell you about how the doctor would listen sympathetically to them and suggest they have another week off work and then have a chat with them about the 'ould country'.

«««««««««««««»»»»»»»»»»»»»

My Uncle Jim was sat on an East Kent bus travelling from Sandwich to Deal. When the bus reached the bus stop near Sandwich railway station, a young fellow got on the bus and sat in front of Uncle Jim. Uncle Jim recognised him as the son of a mining family who lived in the Betteshanger village.

My uncle decided not to engage the young chap in conversation because the young fellow was on his holidays from university and was dressed accordingly in the style of the intelligentsia of the time.

Oxford bags, long scarves wrapped round their necks a couple of times and thrown nonchantly over their backs and long floppy hair that they kept flicking back. In this day and age anybody behaving like that would be dubbed a **** (right prat).

The bus conductor approached the young buck and said **"Fares please!"**

The bright chap said **"Well actually old chap I'm afraid you will have to help me out there, I'm looking for a miners settlement called Bettes something or other, have you any idea where that might be?"**

Before the bus conductor could answer, a disgusted Uncle Jim said **"YOU SHOULD KNOW YOU STUCK UP YOUNG SOD. YOU HAVE LIVED THERE FOR YEARS!"**

«««««««««««««»»»»»»»»»»»»»

Tommy came from Lancashire and was as dry as they come with his wit. He always chewed tobacco and used to amaze us young haulage lads with his unerring accuracy with tobacco juice. He could hit a black clock from twelve feet away very easily. The stories he would tell us about when he first moved down to Kent would have us in stitches.

My favourite one was when he arrived at Snowdown, was given a job and looked around for some digs. He heard about a couple with a cottage in Nonington who took in lodgers. He was accepted as their lodger and moved in.

It was a regular story from miners who took lodgings in this part of Kent in the early days of the Kent Coalfield, before they brought their families down and housed them, that although the digs were spotlessly clean there was never enough food put on the table. There were always flowers on the table, and like Tommy said **"If you could eat flowers I would have been as fat as a pig."**

But to get back to the story, Tommy went to the local pub on Saturday night and after having a good drink he made his way back to his digs. His landlady was setting the table for Sunday breakfast the following morning and said to Tommy **"I will be doing bacon for breakfast, how do you like you bacon done?"**
As quick as a flash Tommy replied **"WITH THREE FRIED EGGS LUV!"**

««««««««««««««»»»»»»»»»»»»»

Tommy soon established himself in the area and after a while was well in demand as the MC at the local dances. One evening while watching the dancers from the stage, out of the corner of his eye he spotted a young fellow sneak past the doorman without paying.
When the music stopped, Tommy called out **"Ladies and Gentlemen we will now have the snake dance. YON BUGGER WHO JUST SNAKED IN WITHOUT PAYING CAN BLOODY WELL SNAKE OUT AGAIN!"**

««««««««««««««»»»»»»»»»»»»»

Tommy's job was taking trainees who had just started working at all the Kent pits from the training centre in Betteshanger down the pit to acclimatise them to working on the haulage system and would ask some of the haulage lads to let the trainees have a go at using the lashing chains or using haulage clips.

There was one trainee Tommy could not get on with. Why this certain trainee chose to work at the mines was a mystery, because he was always dusting himself down, or if he touched a lashing chain or haulage clip he would rub his hands vigorously to get the dust off.

One day this trainee was stood in the pit bottom with the other trainees and he was wearing white cotton gloves. Tommy was eyeing the lad up, when all of a sudden he took a comb out of his pocket, took off his pit helmet and started to comb his hair. This was more than Tommy could stand, and said **"WHO DO YOU THINK YOU ARE? RUDOLF F**KING VALENTINO?!"**

«««««««««««««»»»»»»»»»»»»»

Old doctor Fraser being one of the pit doctors, would sometimes spend a morning over at Betteshanger checking the new intakes of trainees. Tommy would usher the lads in one at a time to see the Doc, and make sure the trainees would behave themselves and keep reasonably quiet.

On one occasion after the Doc had seen to the trainees, he looked at Tommy who he always enjoyed a bit of banter with and noticed that Tommy had been quieter than usual and enquired **"You feeling alright Tommy?"**

"No doctor" replied Tommy **"I've had the guts ache for the last three days."**

"Are you constipated?" asked the doctor.

"No Church of England" said Tommy.

"You know what I mean" said the doctor **"Have you passed anything this morning?"**

"Aye local bobby on his bicycle and two nuns waiting at the bus stop."

Doctor Fraser was actually enjoying all this banter and keeping a straight face said to Tommy **"Have you been moved?"** still referring to Tommy's bowel movement.

"When me mother died I was heartbroken" said Tommy in his broad Lancashire accent.

"For the last time Tommy have you had a st?"** said Doc.

Tommy pretended to sniff the air a couple of times and with a twinkle in his eye said **"IT'S THEE IF ANY BUGGER!"**

«««««««««««««»»»»»»»»»»»»»

You know whenever there is a get together such as a wedding or a celebration wherever people meet to enjoy themselves and have a good time, you always get one or two who make an arse of themselves.

One such night when Tommy was the MC, a couple who no doubt had been overdoing the booze went onto the dance floor where the dancers were enjoying the music and kept bumping into the other dancers by trying to execute some fancy dance steps.

At the end of a waltz where the bloke fell flat on his face, Tommy called out **"Thank you ladies and gents, please clear the floor for the next dance and thank you Fred Rogers and Ginger Astaire."**
One or two of the people there called out **"Don't you mean Fred Astaire and Ginger Rogers, Tommy?"**
"I know who I am talking about!" replied Tommy with a disgusted look at the boozed up couple.

«««««««««««««»»»»»»»»»»»»»

I remember once looking at a photograph from the nineteen thirties where all these Kent miners were attending a union meeting all dressed in their Sunday best. It seemed the dress of the day was flat caps, short jackets, drain pipe trousers and white silk scarves knotted tightly around their necks.

I asked this miner who was in the photograph why they tied their scarves so tight and he informed me that at the time that the photograph was taken they had been on strike for a couple of weeks and they did not want the pit bosses to think they were going hungry, so they made their scarves tight around their necks to make their faces red, so that it would look as though they had eaten a hearty breakfast (Ask a silly question).

«««««««««««««»»»»»»»»»»»»»

My Grandad B and Granny B once spent a Saturday afternoon in Dover in the early thirties doing some shopping and afterwards thought it would be nice to round off the visit by treating themselves to a meal in one of the restaurants. The one they chose was rather toffology with silver service and waiters done up like penguins.

My grandad was rather taken up with a gent who was sat at the next table, who would not have looked out of place at the Lord Mayors banquet. After ordering off the menu, the waiter who was serving them asked my grandad **"Would you like a serviette sir?"**

Grandad in typical Derbyshire fashion replied **"IF YON BUGGER CAN EAT ONE"** nodding towards the gent at the next table **"SO CAN I!"**

«««««««««««««»»»»»»»»»»»»»

A well known large Scottish family who lived in Mill Hill were gathered around their father's bed and poor old Wullie was about to pop his clogs. His six sons went downstairs to discuss the funeral when it happened. Just as they were about to speak Old Wullie rallied round and could hear the conversation.

It started with the oldest son saying **"Ye Ken the funeral's going to cost us all a lot of money"**, to which one of the other sons suggested that, maybe there were ways in which they could cut costs.

One son suggested that they should buy the cheapest coffin there was. Another son said **"Why not request no flowers? that should save them some money."**

Then came the thing they were all dreading. The cost of the hearse and taxis.

The youngest son said **"Seeing as Hamilton Road Cemetery was only a half mile down the road, why don't they take turns carrying the coffin to the cemetery?"**

This was more than Old Wullie could stand and shouted angrily **"HEY YOUSE LOT. IF YOUSE BRING MY TROOSERS UP I'LL F**KING WALK DOON THERE!"**

THE WAR YEARS

During the Second World War, quite a few Kent miners joined the Home Guards and whereas most of them took it seriously, some thought it was a waste of time and joined just for a laugh.

On one occasion a regular army officer was giving a lecture on battle tactics to a platoon of Home Guards at the old Drill Hall in Middle Deal Road.

The Officer pointed to one of the Home Guards who originally came from Yorkshire and worked at Betteshanger and said **"Now imagine you are in command of all the British army in Kent and the Germans invade Deal, what steps would you take?"**

"Bloody great long ones" replied the miner **"AND DIG IT AT DONNY!"** (Doncaster)

«««««««««««««»»»»»»»»»»»»»

Three admirals were stood on the deck of the HMS Victory at Portsmouth, just after the Second World War. One was Russian, the second was American and the third was British.

They each had with them their batman, or the equivalent of what they were called in the Navy. The three admirals were having a discussion on who's sailors were the bravest. The Russian admiral was adamant that Russian sailors were the bravest and said **"Watch this"** and turning to his sailor said **"Ivan climb up to the first yardarm and dive onto the deck."**

Ivan jumped to attention, saluted and said **"Ja Comrade Admiral"**, ran smartly over to the mast, climbed nimbly up to the first yardarm and dived head first onto the deck breaking both arms and knocking himself unconscious. **"What is more braver than that?"** said the Russian admiral.

Not to be outdone the American admiral said to his all American type sailor **"Chuck climb up to the second yardarm and dive head first onto the deck."**
"Sure thing admiral" said Chuck and ambled over to the main mast like John Wayne, each step flexing his bulging muscles.

On reaching the second yardarm Chuck dived head first onto the deck breaking both arms and both legs and fracturing his skull. **"What is braver than that?"** said the American admiral.

The British admiral not to be outdone turned to his sailor who happened to be an ex Kent miner and said **"Rodney old boy be a good chap and climb up to the third yardarm and dive head first into the deck."**
"You go and fk yourself"** said Rodney.
"There" said the British admiral **"WHAT IS BRAVER THAN THAT?!"**

«««««««««««»»»»»»»»»»»

After the shock of Dunkirk in the Second World War the threat of invasion seemed very likely. It was thought that in the event of this happening it would confuse the enemy if all road and street signs were taken down.

On one occasion about three years into the war this caused a dilemma outside the Co-Op at Mill Hill. The story goes that the greengrocer was doing his round with his horse and cart, when the poor horse dropped dead between the shafts, right on the junction of Beauchamp Avenue and Arthur Road. The local bobby was sent for, who at this time happened to be a Special Constable.

On arriving at the scene, the Special Constable who was not the brightest tool in the box asked the small crowd who had gathered there what the name of the street was and because the horse and cart was pointed up Beauchamp Avenue, they told him Beauchamp Avenue.

Now here is where the fun started. He asked how do they spell Beauchamp Avenue. One or two of the locals told the bobby that it was pronounced Beecham, but was not spelt that way. Some of the people had a go at spelling Beauchamp, but they could not agree because of the signs being taken down. A wise old collier came to their rescue and suggested that they turn the horse and cart round and point it up Arthur Road. This was duly done and everyone went home happy.

««««««««««««««»»»»»»»»»»»»»»

Little Jimmy K was a little Scotsman who lived in Betteshanger Village. He was liked and respected by all the men at Betteshanger Colliery, but he was given a wide berth by most women, because Jimmy, no matter how hard he tried, could not string a sentence together without saying the F word or bastard.

The men did not let it bother them when they were working with Jimmy or having a drink with him; because I don't have to tell you how relaxing it can be when you are getting a bit stressed working down the mine and you give the job its pedigree, a few f**ks and other choice of words can make you feel like you can manage whatever the job throws at you!

Jimmy suffered from 'Trench Foot', a horrible complaint from the First World War, caused by having to spend time in trenches, standing in freezing mud up to their knees for days on end. You would often see Jimmy shuffling on his way to the Betteshanger Social Club, which was about as far as he could manage in his latter years.

However, for all the pain Jimmy suffered with his feet, once he made it to the club and had his first pint you could see the gloom and pain lift from him and the twinkle in his eye would tell you that whatever the topic of conversation was, Jimmy would turn it into a pantomime. He would only use the public bar because he knew that he would forget himself if he went into the concert room among the women, and try as he might, he would f**k it up in heaps.

During the height of the 'Battle of Britain', Jimmy was doing a bit of gardening when the air raid sirens sounded. He walked into his house and called upstairs to his wife Sarah, who had just got out of the bath,
"Sarah, get yerself doon here, the Germans are coming."
"Jimmy, I haven't got me knickers on!" Sarah shouted back.
Typical of Jimmy, his response was **"THE JERRIES HAVE COME TO BOMB YE, NOT F**K YE!"**

Another tale about Jimmy was that if he overdid the drinking he would wet the bed. On one of these occasions he was stood on his back door step, the morning after a good session and on the washing line was a big white bed sheet with a big round stain in the middle of it where Jimmy had wet the bed again.

A couple of doors away a woman was hanging out her washing and obviously had seen Jimmy's bed sheet. At that time, Japan had joined the Second World War on the side of Germany, so Jimmy called out to her **"Hey missus' ye see that on the washing line, THAT'S THE FLAG OF JAPAN!"**

Much as Jimmy was accepted by the men of the village, they had to ban him for a while from the Betteshanger Social Club. The reason for this was during the bitter cold winter of early 1940 Jimmy had struggled round to the club. When he walked into the public bar, all the other men there stood four deep round the big pot-bellied stove trying to get warm. Jimmy felt frozen and tried to push his way through, but those around the stove would not budge.

"Let me through ye bastards!" said Jimmy.
Most of the men stood there used Jimmy's favourite word and replied **"F**k off Jimmy!"**

"RIGHT YE BASTARDS, I'LL SHIFT YE!" replied Jimmy and with that he exposed his genitalia and urinated all over the one piece of central heating. It shifted them all right! You could imagine the fragrance permeating the atmosphere. Although a lot of the members had a laugh about it afterwards, they could not let Jimmy get away with such behaviour, so Jimmy was banned for a while.

««««««««««««»»»»»»»»»»»»

One miner I don't mind naming is Dick Sullivan. Dick without a doubt is the funniest person I have ever met. He just seemed to go on forever cracking jokes and telling funny stories.

Dick was well known throughout the Kent Coalfields and beyond because of his love of rugby, and his talent of turning any get together into an occasion people would never forget. Although he had an Irish name he was Welsh, and proud of it.

If you were down the pit or anywhere where Dick was and you could hear laughter, it would be a good bet that Dick was the reason for it. I always remember his version of an old saying was **"He who keeps his head, while those all around are losing theirs, does not realise the gravity of the situation."** As I have hinted, there was a bit of Irish there somewhere.

During the Second World War, Betteshanger miners were forced to make a heart searching decision. The underground area at Betteshanger known as the South East, could not cope with the water constantly dripping through the roof, so the miners decided after negotiations broke down over better working conditions, or extra money while working in such a wet environment, to strike.

With the war at a critical stage, this decision was not taken lightly. While negotiations were going on to get the miners back to work and to come to some arrangement, it was decided to get the mine owners to come down and see what the problem was. When a party of mine owners, union reps and a certain collier from the coalface arrived at the scene of the trouble, all they could see was about four foot of water as far as the eye could see. A large raft had been built of pit props to ferry the party along the workings.

Whilst propelling themselves along by various means, one of the mine owners noticed a lot of bubbles coming to the surface of the water. It was probably an air pipe leaking, but when he enquired what it was, Dick Sullivan who was the collier representing the coalface workers said **"Oh that's one of the maintenance men putting his tools away!"**

«««««««««««««»»»»»»»»»»»»»

I remember once asking Dick why he had suddenly stopped using the 'Yew Tree' pub at the top of Mill Hill, which was only yards away from where he lived. Dick told me that Fred the Landlord who was one of the tightest buggers he had ever met, asked Dick one day if he knew any new jokes. This gave Dick a chance to pull the landlords leg.

The joke Dick told in front of a full public bar did not go down well with Fred the landlord and this is how it went, an old miner who lived in Mill Hill died and landed at the Pearly Gates. The angel Peter looked at him and said **"We are not ready for you yet. Fly back down to Deal beach and count all the pebbles between Sandown Castle and Deal Pier and we will probably be ready for you."**

Off the old miner flew and returned five years later and told Peter how many pebbles there were between Sandown Castle and Deal Pier. "**I am sorry**" said Peter "**But we are still not ready for you yet, fly back down to Deal and count how many blades of grass there are on Deal golf course.**"

So off the old miner flew and after another five years returned and told Peter how many blades of grass there were on Deal golf course. The angel Peter was still not ready to let the old miner into heaven, so he had to think up something that would keep the old miner down on earth for a very long time.

Suddenly Peter had a brilliant idea. "**I know what you can do**" said Peter to the old miner "**Go down to the Yew Tree pub at the top of Mill Hill and stand at the public bar and wait for Fred the landlord to give you a free pint of beer!**"

The roars of laughter from the rest of the customers so annoyed Fred that he would not serve Dick any more so Dick decided to do his drinking elsewhere.

««««««««««««««»»»»»»»»»»»»»»

At the latter half of the Second World War, if any older people can remember, there was a story about a young soldier stationed at Dover Castle who, while on guard duty one very dark night, believed he saw a headless drummer slowly marching along playing his drum.

The story goes that the young soldier on guard was so frightened that his hair turned white overnight. This story which was published in all the papers at the time rekindled the debate about whether there were ghosts or not. None more so than in the Kent mining community and this brings me to a story that was told a few years after the event.

Apparently a group of Kent miners were having a discussion in their club about ghosts and one miner made it quite clear that he did not believe in ghosts and when one of his mates bet him five pounds (and in those days that was nearly a weeks wages) that he would not stay in Dover Castle on his own for one night, would he do it. After many pints of Kent's finest brews, he felt ready to face the devil himself. He agreed to do it and the arrangements were made. The miner in question arrived at Dover Castle and was locked inside for the night.

Everything went well at first, the miner felt bored and fell asleep on a bed that had been made up for him, in a room near the castle gate. On the stroke of midnight something disturbed him and he woke with a start. He was aware of a presence in the room where he was and called out **"Is anybody there?"**
A ghostly voice replied **"There's only me and thee."**
Our miner friend was scared witless and shot out of the door and bolted towards the castle gate and shouted back **"IF I CAN GET THROUGH THIS BLOODY GATE THERE WILL ONLY BE THEE!"**

«««««««««««««»»»»»»»»»»»»»

A person I must mention is Twinkletoes, or Joey Twinkletoes as some called him. Joey worked at Betteshanger and played football for Betteshanger football team. Joey was a natural left footer and played on the left wing, as it was called in years gone by. When Joey got the ball on his left foot he could weave magic with it and could send inch perfect crosses with it from the left wing, but if the ball was put on his right foot he was useless to say the least. Perhaps this was the reason he never progressed any higher than the Kent league.

Someone once said that if Twinkletoes was passed the ball on his right foot he had to go out of the Welfare ground, down Davis Avenue, up Redsull Avenue and along Douglas Road before he could get it on to his left foot. If you are wondering what all this is building up to, it is to tell you about the only goal he was known to have scored.

Twinkletoes' footballing career was mainly played through the Second World War years and just after. The 1944 season had only been going a couple of weeks when this country was being attacked by VI guided missiles, or doodlebugs as they were commonly known, and a match was being played on the Welfare ground at Mill Hill between Betteshanger and another team, probably one of the many army teams that were stationed in this area at the time.

Apparently the game was well under way, when all of a sudden the rapid chug chug of a doodlebug could be heard approaching from the direction of Kingsdown. All the time you could hear that chug chug sound you knew you were safe, but when it started to cut out or stop, that was the time to dive for cover, or lay flat and cover your head with your hands.

The doodlebug seemed to be only about half a mile away when it started to splutter and cut out. Everybody including the many spectators who used to watch the football in those days, plus the two teams, the referee and the two linesmen lay flat. All that is except Twinkletoes who had just been passed the ball on the left wing. Twinkletoes made for the goal and tapped it in to the goal.

The doodlebug suddenly started to pick up again and resumed its normal chug chug sound and carried on its way. Everybody slowly stood up again and the referee realised he had not blown the whistle, had to concede that Joey had indeed scored a goal. That was the only goal Joey Twinkletoes ever scored at that level.

«««««««««««««»»»»»»»»»»»»

When the Second World War came to an end, my uncle Jim who had always kept pigeons, was looking forward to racing his pigeons again and one race he had in mind was racing them from France. He assumed that it was only a matter of time before the races from France would start up again, so he thought he would get in early and get his pigeons used to the last part of the route.

Because we lived in Betteshanger village, Uncle Jim decided to send cousin Bill, his son, who is still a very keen pigeon man, my older brother Charlie and myself, on our bikes one Sunday morning with baskets of pigeons tied on the back, to Whitfield Hill. We were told by uncle Jim to take the pigeons half way down the hill, take the baskets into a field and let the pigeons go. This we did and the pigeons flew off in the direction of Betteshanger.

After tying the baskets back on our bikes we started back on our journey home. I shall always remember remarking to Charlie and Bill when we had only got to the top of Whitfield Hill **"I bet the pigeons are already back at Betteshanger eating their corn!"**

Would you believe it, they never turned up until Wednesday evening.

«««««««««««««»»»»»»»»»»»»»

I remember a very keen pigeon fancier who lived in the circle at Betteshanger who, when the Second World War ended, like a lot of other people wanted to get back to some semblance of how life had been before the long dreary years of war.

This fellow Frank, held a very important job on the pit top. He was a nice enough guy six days a week, but on a Saturday afternoon when he was waiting to clock his pigeons in from a race, God help you if you made a noise, or were stood in a back garden within fifty yards of his pigeon shed.

It was known if people were talking in the street in front of his house, when he was waiting for his pigeons to come home from a race Frank would walk down to the front gate and ask them politely but firmly to move on.

When the pigeons made an appearance if they did not fly straight into the shed and let Frank get their rings off their legs and clock them in as quick as possible, he would get a tin with some corn in and rattle it to try and coax the bird off the roof of the house or shed. We the neighbours would sit back and listen to the performance with a smile because we knew what to expect.

It used to go like this:

"Come on my old duck. Come on my little beauty, lets be having you sweetheart."

Then you would hear Frank starting to get a bit frustrated as the pigeon ignored him.

""**Get down here you bloody thing!**" Frank would say with menace creeping into his voice.

If there was still no response from the pigeon you would hear Frank rattling the tin a bit harder and his voice getting more angry. Then came the explosion we knew would come. 'Crash' would go the tin with the corn in as Frank would throw it down on the ground in a rage. Then you would hear Frank giving the pigeon its ancestry.

"You bugger, you bloody rotten bugger, I don't know why I bloody well bother with you, you bloody sodding little buggers!"

This could be heard all over Betteshanger village. Then you would hear Frank's wife, a nice dear person come to the back door and say **"Frank for goodness sake come in here, what do you think the neighbours will think of you going on like that!"**
If Frank was really angry and frustrated at seeing his chances of winning the pigeon race diminishing you'd hear Frank say to his wife **"BUGGER THE NEIGHBOURS!"**

«««««««««««««»»»»»»»»»»»»»

No story of the Kent miners would be complete if it did not mention the term 'Cock Wood'.

This was related to a piece of timber sawn from a pit prop and then taken home and chopped up for fire wood, so that the coal fires could be made. It was generally accepted that if a miner regularly took home a nice bit of pine with a straight grain that was easy for his wife to chop, he would get his regular bit of 'nookie'. If he did not take home a lump of 'cock wood', his wife would refuse him his nuptials.

I know of one family (not a million miles away) who had one son who had just finished his training to go down the pit. He was working on the haulage just in from the pit bottom and noticed some of the older haulage lads and light workmen sawing bits of wood off the end of pit props, that were waiting to be sent into the coalfaces and asked one of the light workmen what they were doing.

"Sawing up cock wood to take home" said the old fellow.
"What's cock wood?" asked the young lad.
"Just another name for fire wood" replied the old chap, who did not bother to explain any further.

The young lad thought 'I think I'll take a bit of cock wood home' and sawed himself a nice piece of pine off a pit prop. He took the cock wood home and when he walked into the house; his mother had just put the dinner on the table for his father and two older brothers, who were tucking into their meals. The lad handed the bit of wood to his mother and said **"I've brought some cock wood home, mum."**

His dad dropped the knife and fork, one brother nearly choked on a piece of potato and the other brother's mouth fell open wide allowing gravy to run down his chin and onto his shirt front. The lad's mum being knowledgeable to the slang and jargon of the miners said **"Dad, take him outside and explain to him what it means!"**

After the initial shock, the father and the two sons fell about with helpless laughter.

Betteshanger Colliery ended up employing a security man after the Second World War and the man they employed had been a special constable during the war. He was treated with suspicion by ninety-nine per cent of the pit workers, because during the war it seemed every week his name would appear in the East Kent Mercury where he had arrested someone for riding a bike without a rear-light at night.

Every now and again, he would walk around the pithead baths and confiscate any cock wood he saw. Miners coming up the pit would be warned by pit top men he was on the prowl.

One miner, Andy, who had gone through the First World War fighting in France in one of the Scottish regiments and feared neither man or beast, walked into the pithead baths with a lump of cock wood under his arm and was met by the 'Pit Bobby', who said **"I'll take that piece of wood if you don't mind."**

"Aye, I do mind" said Andy **"So f**k off!"**

"You'll get me shot if I let you take that wood home" said the Pit Bobby, a bit taken aback by Andy's abrupt reply.

"You should have been shot long ago!" said Andy and carried on, onto his locker.

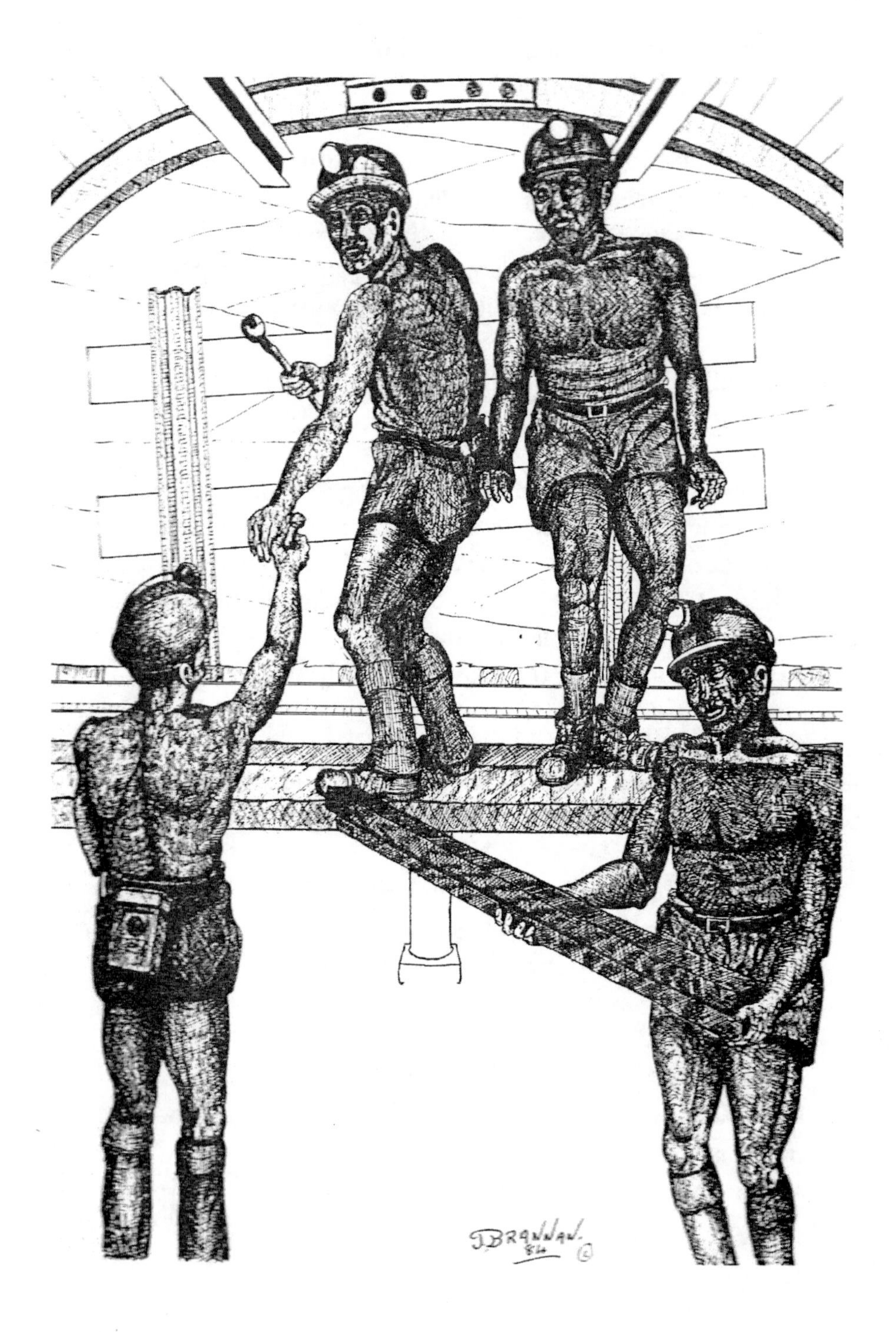
J.BRANNAN.
'86

ON THE COALFACE

I recall as a young lad in the early nineteen fifties doing my coalface training on a hand got coalface and any older miner does not have to be reminded what a shock it was to the system.

You were not spared the tortuous muscle aching agony to your body until you got used to it. The thing was, your pride would not let you give up because if your mates and relations had done it, you did not want them to think you were soft.

You were usually put with an experienced collier, who no doubt knew what your body and mind were going through, but had to push you a bit harder each day, until you could match him and perhaps even pull his leg and say something like **"Not feeling very energetic today John?"** or **"You want to leave it alone during the week Arthur or you will be ending up with Shaggers Back!"**.

This usually provoked an answer like **"I CAN STILL LEAVE YOU STANDING YOU CHEEKY YOUNG SOD!"**

I can remember that time when you'd finished your shift and were making your way out to the pit bottom, or waiting to go up in the cage, and perhaps some of the timber or haulage lads were skylarking about. A favourite saying of the colliers and rippers was **"IT'S SOME WORK YOU BUGGERS WANT!"** Once I finished my training I went to work on the coalface.

THE DAY SHIFT (Six 'til Two)

The pit buses pulled up outside the pithead baths and one by one the men stepped off and wandered into the canteen. In the canteen, the canteen ladies quickly and efficiently served them their cups of tea and whatever snacks they required, because there was no time for hanging around.

The last ride down the pit, left the pit top at 6.30am and the last drag on a half smoked ciggie was then flicked away as the men and lads, still adjusting their hat lamps made their way over to the pit shaft with their various coalface teams, or perhaps a bunch of haulage lads who had been hanging about were given a not so gentle reminder by an overman or even an undermanager to get their arses down the pit before he sent them back home.

Stood on the pit bank crammed together, the underground men would not say a lot, because they would be watching the Banksman who operated the signals and levers that brought the cage to the right level, so that those riding the shaft could board the cage.

Heading men would be carrying one or two heavy powder cans filled with explosives. No one offered to help the heading men to carry the powder cases, but on some coal faces where they ran a rota of letting the team take turns of riding the pit an hour early, taking out the empty powder cans, you might get one of the colliers say **"Want a hand with them pal?"** (Might)

This concession of getting an early ride up the pit felt like a prisoner suddenly being told he does not have to do the rest of his sentence.

But back to the men waiting to go down the pit. Once you were loaded on to the cage, you knew that was it for the next seven and half hours, so you usually had a chat with the chap next to you. Hearing the different accents, Geordie, Lanc, Scot, Cherry Picker, Taffy, Cockingese, Irish, you are reminded of a debate by the assembly of the United Nations.

Stepping off the cage at the pit bottom, you will probably see some bleary eyed nightshift men who had to stay on until they were relieved by day shift men. Especially the pump men. Deputies and chargehands would quickly get their teams together and let them know if there was anything they should know about their coalface or heading and if any of the team had not turned up, so that they could get a Market man, (these were trained colliers and heading men who for some reason did not have a regular team to work with).

The next thing was to make your way to the paddy, or manrider and journey in to the district where you worked. On arrival at your coalface or heading you did not hang around if you were on contract and bonus, because you learnt from your chargehand what coalface team was trying and what coalface team was not, but when the conditions and opportunity was there to make good money everybody seemed to give it all they had got.

'Snaptime' (halftime break) was always looked forward to, so you could have the machinery turned off for twenty minutes and sit down and eat what you had brought from home, plus drink your tea or coffee if you had brought a flask. If not, you drank from your water bottle. This was a good time to catch up with the local gossip, or pontificate on the world situation, or generally extract the urine from one of the team who's turn it was to have his private life hung out to dry, or even have things made up about him.

With the resumption of work after 'snaptime' it would depend how the work was going whether the time went quickly or slowly. It was always better if the time went quickly, in spite of your efforts to keep your end up and not leave too much for your mates on the afternoon shift.

When the time came to leave the job, you felt that a weight had been lifted from your shoulders and in spite of your aches and pains and tiredness you could not wait to get down to the paddy/manrider to start your journey to the pit bottom and eventually back home.

At the pit bottom you will no doubt meet your opposite number, on the afternoon shift and quickly fill him in on any details about the job and enquire about the weather, then wish him a pleasant shift and tell him you will think of him after you have had your lunch and just about to have a nap in the armchair.

On arrival at the pit top you leave your cap lamp in the lamp cabin and make your way to the pithead baths and depending on what kind of a shift you have had, you either go to your clean locker, get a cigarette, light up and walk back to your dirty locker and take your time getting ready for a shower if you have had a grueller, or make a dash for it, and get one of the good showers, if you still have a modicum of energy left.

After a refreshing shower and getting dressed, it's back into the canteen for a lovely cup of tea, or whatever your choice of refreshment is and a very nice meal if you cannot wait until you get home or one of the meat pies that I had to force myself to ignore as I passed them.

Depending on whether you had your own transport or used the pit buses, looking at the countryside on your way home made you really glad, especially if it were summertime, because in all my travels nowhere beats Kent for scenery.

«««««««««««««»»»»»»»»»»»»»

If you started down the pit when you left school years ago, you started as a haulage lad and worked around the pit bottom, sending empty tubs or mine cars into the coalfaces, plus materials and took part in sending coal to the surface.

You could progress to being a timber lad. This meant you went further into the workings and unloaded pit props and other materials near the coalface and when the colliers wanted the pit props and other means of support, you and the other timber lads would send the required timber and whatever else was required down the coalface.

This job was the next stage to becoming a coalface worker. It was a higher paid job than being an ordinary haulage lad and as the colliers on the coalface were on contract, if you kept them well supplied and they made a good wage and bonus, the charge hand would go round with the hat and make it all worth your while. Like most of the workers in the pit if you were on an hourly wage and not on contract you tended to watch the clock.

One Friday the timber lads, on one coalface were itching to get away and were gathering their things together so they could dash to the pit bottom and get the first cage up the pit. As luck would have it, the district overman came off the coalface and stopped them from dashing off. There was about six mine cars with three foot props and four foot props that had not been unloaded.

The overman said to the timer lads **"Make yourselves useful, I want you to unload these mine cars and put the three foot props on the left and the four foot props on the right."**

"I know what you fking want!"** replied a timber lad to himself, but not soft enough.
"Oh, and what do I fking want?!"** asked the overman.

"Three foot props on the left and four foot props on the right!" replied the timber lad.

«««««««««««»»»»»»»»»»»

After a spell in the army I returned to work at Betteshanger in the mid fifties and had the pleasure of working on the pit top repairing mine cars with this quiet but very funny Scotsman, who was called Jock, for obvious reasons.

Although Jock rarely smiled he would come out with some real gems. I learnt after a while when one of these gems was about to be delivered, because he would slowly close his left eye and the corners of his mouth would twitch.

One Monday morning, I noticed that at times Jock was actually smiling to himself. After a while I could stand it no longer and said **"Come on Jock lets hear it!"** He was almost reluctant to tell me, but he eventually closed that left eye and the mouth twitched.

The story he told me had happened the weekend just past. Apparently Jock and his next door neighbour were doing a bit of gardening at their houses in Mill Hill on the Saturday morning and they stopped for a chat. As with most men 'subject normal', or sex as it is referred to now, came up.

Jocks next door neighbour confided in Jock that his love life was virtually non existent. Jock the devil that he was told his neighbour that he performed two or three times a week and his secret was to go to the Welfare Club and down ten pints of Shepherd Neame's best bitter. We can only assume that Jock's neighbour took anything Jock told him as gospel.

The following morning (Sunday) Jock got up early to make his wife and himself a cup of tea and spotted his neighbour in the back garden pegging bed sheets on the washing line. Opening the kitchen window,

Jock called out, **"You're up early this morning!"** Jock's neighbour glared at him and gave Jock the father of all boll**kings.

Apparently Jock's neighbour took the rascally Jock at his word and went out Saturday night to the Welfare Club and did his best to follow Jocks advice to improve his sexual performance, got blind drunk, had to be carried home, put to bed and woke in the morning to find he had s**t the bed!

««««««««««««»»»»»»»»»»»

Jock related a story to me one day about a fellow Scot called Fergie.

Before the pits were nationalised and the five day week was brought in, it was compulsory to work Saturdays.

Fergie worked one Saturday morning and had to stop on a bit longer than usual. When he got back to his digs in Deal, where he lodged with three other miners, there was not a soul to be seen.

He was starving hungry and the landlady had gone shopping, so he started looking round for something to eat and entering the kitchen he found a pot of stew the landlady had made, simmering on the stove.

He got a spoon and decided to help himself to a few mouthfuls. It tasted so nice Fergie forgot when to stop and before he realised what he was doing, the stew was almost gone. Fergie knew if he was caught there, he would be chucked out of his digs and as digs go they were the best, so he dashed out and went to the cinema for a few hours.

When he made his way back to his digs and entering the house noticed an atmosphere that could be cut with a knife. The other three who lodged there were looking a bit annoyed and sorry for themselves. Fergie with a look on his face as though butter would not melt in his mouth, asked if something was wrong.

The landlady asked Fergie if he had been in the house that afternoon, while she had been out shopping because someone, she said, glaring angrily at the other three lodgers had been in and ate most of the stew.

Straight faced Fergie claimed to have just finished working overtime at Betteshanger and said he was as hungry as hell. The landlady said she would cook Fergie some bacon and eggs but the other three would get nothing. While the other three lodgers looked on, Fergie ate his bacon and eggs, Fergie kept up his air of innocence and had the nerve to chastise them.

Before I consign Jock to history I would like to mention a time Jock and I were having a drink together in the Magnet pub at Upper Deal one Saturday lunchtime. It was his favourite pub and after buying one another a drink each, Jock lowered his voice and told me to move over to the corner, where we could not be seen from the bar. I guessed my education was about to receive a golden lesson that no university could rival.

On the wall in the corner was a pin-ball machine that when you dropped a penny in the slot, a ball dropped down and you pressed down a handle and let it go and the ball would fly round the machine a couple of times with the object of falling into one of five protruding channels which would give you another free go plus your penny back.

Needless to say the maker of these machines built them so that the chances of you getting a free go and your penny back were minimal. Jock being the shrewd Scot that he was had worked out a method of shortening the odds.

By placing his thumb on the small knob jutting out from the machine and pressing the lever on to his thumb and letting the lever go, the ball would go round only once slowly and would drop into one of the channels. I stood there and watched him drop out enough pennies to buy us another pint each. I can only assume whoever owned the machine must have thought somebody had been very lucky.

«««««««««««««»»»»»»»»»»»»»

If ever you got a Lancashire man and a Yorkshire man together, it was certain the old war of the roses would surface, not may I add in animosity, but in good natured banter.

Lanc and this Yorkshire man were bragging about what was the best between Lancashire Hot Pot and Yorkshire Pudding. After singing the praises of Lancashire Hot Pot by Lanc, Albert a 'reet' Yorkshire lad, started to reveal the secrets of a good Yorkshire pudding. According to Albert, you did not just throw flour, eggs, milk into a bowl and mix it, but you had to stir it with love and affection.

"Tell me again" said Lanc **"What is in the mixture?"**
Albert repeated the recipe and Lanc said **"WE USED THAT FOR PAPERING WALLS IN LANCASHIRE!"**

«««««««««««««»»»»»»»»»»»»»

I think the dirtiest job on the pit top in years gone by was working on what was called the 'Screens'.

This job was where the tubs of coal were tipped into a hopper, which in turn fed conveyor belts and men and boys would pick out any lumps of rock from the coal going by. The segregated coal would then go on to be sold to the various markets. As I have mentioned it was a very dirty and dusty job and at the time I worked there, they did not even have water sprayers to keep the dust down.

This reminds me of a story where Deal Hospital received an accident from Betteshanger Colliery. The scene is set in the Outpatients department. A man is laid on a stretcher unconscious completely naked and covered from head to toe in thick coal dust, except for his todger, which is completely clean.

The doctor on duty at the time was a very famous doctor who was decorated for his bravery tending to sailors who were injured at sea. He was also one of the pit doctors and sizing up the situation said to the sister there **"Now then sister, a mine worker covered in coal dust except for his private parts, what does it tell you about him?!"**

The sister confessed that she did not have a clue. The doctor with a smile informed her that in his opinion the man worked on the 'Screens' on the pit top and that he also lived in the village by the pit and had probably been home for 'snaptime' before he had his accident.

««««««««««««»»»»»»»»»»»»

This lad called Dicky had a right big hooter on him and I remember one day we were assembling a crossing on the pit top, getting it ready to send down the pit for the Paddy road.

We had worked through 'snaptime' and eventually got the crossing loaded and over to the pit shaft ready to go down the pit. Dicky had been giving us road layers a hand and suggested we go to the fitters shop where there was some seats so that we could sit down for our break.

We did this and once we were all settled, Dicky opened his sandwich box, took out a large apple and started to munch away. Cyril, the fitting shop foreman, looked over at Dicky and said **"It can't be easy not being able to see what you are eating Dicky."**

For a moment Dicky stopped munching and then realising Cyril was referring to the size of his nose almost choked on his apple and spluttered **"You cheeky bastard!"**

Another lad who had a large nose was Big Jack. When I say Jack was big, I don't mean he was brawny but he stood at least six foot four and seemed to loom over everybody.

His nose was long and thin and one bitterly cold morning when he was waiting for the pit bus to get to work, a fellow miner noticed that Jack had a dewdrop hanging from his nose and said **"Jack wipe that dripper from your nose."**

Jack replied **"THEE WIPE IT, THA'S NEAREST!"**

««««««««««««»»»»»»»»»»»»

An overman from Staffordshire was telling some haulage lads about how high the coalfaces were in Staffordshire. This overman was prone to exaggeration somewhat, and if you had a black can he had a blacker one.

He told the haulage lads that it was nothing to see coalfaces as much as 80 feet high in Staffordshire. As any experienced collier will know, one way of testing the roof in the old days was to tap it with a pick shaft, and if it made a ringing noise it was considered safe. If it did not, it should be supported with timber as soon as possible.

One young haulage lad asked the overman how, then, did they test the roof if it was so high? The overman, who was never stuck for an answer, replied that the deputies carried a catapult, and a small bag of marbles, and used to fire them up at the roof and listen for a ringing sound!

I remember as a young teenager, when working in the blacksmiths shop before going down the pit, helping the blacksmiths every now and then making steel wedges. These were used by the colliers to drive into cracks in the hard coal, and would help to make the coal break away from the coal face, and be easier to use their picks and shovels on.

The overman from Staffordshire told us about one occasion where a collier was working on one of the high coal faces up on a ladder. The collier was about thirty foot off the floor and was using one of those steel wedges, which was about two foot long. When driven into the coalface with a sledgehammer it kept falling out, and he had to keep going back down the ladder to retrieve it.

Suddenly he had a great idea - why not get a piece of rope and tie one end to the wedge and the other end round his neck. Then if the wedge came out of the coal, all he had to do would be to pull the rope up and put the wedge back in the crack. He did this and knocked the wedge into the coalface, and fell off the ladder and hung himself!

«««««««««««»»»»»»»»»»»

The usual image of miners is one of tough macho guys who work hard and play hard, so you can imagine what they thought when in the nineteen fifties there were a few limp wristed persons to be seen around the mine.

Two such persons were Freddy and Jacky, or Freda and Jacqueline to give them their pit names. Jacqueline was a bit dull but Freda had a razor sharp wit and anybody who tried to verbally abuse him, or take the mickey out of him, always came a very poor second.

One such chap who started calling Freda names and giving his opinion of what he thought of Freda and his kind in a crowded pit bottom one morning, did not know where to put himself when Freda replied **"You did not say that yesterday in the showers when you wanted to borrow my pink Camay soap!"**

The management seemed to despair of where to send Freda, because everywhere they sent him to work, the job would come to a halt when Freda started telling jokes and making camp innuendos. One day though, he was not in such a good mood because where he and Jacqueline lived someone had stuck a notice in their front garden which read **'Fred and Breakfast ten and six!'**

Of all the jokes about this pair the one that sticks in my mind is when they both went to Blackpool on holiday and Freda was dying to have a go on the 'Big Dipper'. No doubt the very name conjured up a picture of all he desired. Jacqueline did not have the spirit of adventure like Freda and declined. Freda, however, paid his fare and went on the Big Dipper and Jacqueline stayed to watch.

When the ride was over, Freda got off the Big Dipper and tripped and fell down the six steps to where Jacqueline was stood and landed at his feet.

Naturally Jacqueline was very concerned for his friend and helping Freda to his feet asked **"Are you hurt?"**

Freda, as camp as ever, replied **"Of course I am hurt, three times I waved to you going round and you never waved back!"**

««««««««««««««»»»»»»»»»»»»»

A group of young miners were having a drink in a pub in Deal and they started talking shop. They were discussing the development of a new coalface and one of the young miners mentioned that the Endless Belt would have to be extended (an Endless Belt is another name for a conveyor belt).

A young barman who knew the young miners asked "What is an Endless Belt?" Freda, who was also listening to the conversation and fancied the young barman, said **"A LONG WEEKEND WITH ME DUCKEE!"**

«««««««««««««»»»»»»»»»»»»»

Robbo was also a haulage deputy at Betteshanger and like a good general in the army always led from the front. He always set an example and if you were on his district he would stay with you and made sure you learned the job you were on until you felt confident. He also had a mischievous streak in him and he would set someone up for a piss-take (if you will pardon the expression).

There was this lad called Arnold who had taken up boxing and though Arnold trained very hard and looked like a boxer his record was not very inspiring. Whenever he was due to fight, his enthusiasm and dedication was a hundred and ten per cent and in a way being a regular guy we really wished him luck, but usually the day after he had a fight I and the rest of the haulage lads would know by his glum silence that things had not gone to plan.

Robbo however was less diplomatic and would usually size up the situation and say **"Second prize again last night Arnold."** This usually defused the situation and Arnold's face would break into a grin and he would be the happy go lucky Arnold we liked to see.

I got to know Robbo and could usually tell when he was cooking something up because when things were a bit slack on the job, he could invent silly kind of games which seemed to make the time go quicker.

He started this game where he would sit about six haulage lads in a circle and would put a rubber ring in the middle. This rubber ring was about six inches in diameter and Robbo would in turn hand us a miners pick and tell us to close our eyes and see how many times we could get the point of the pick in the rubber ring. After a while everybody seemed to be able to do it six times out of six.

Robbo claimed we were all cheating and opening our eyes. We all denied this and Robbo put the next part of his plan into operation. He said if we agreed to be blindfolded and do it he would believe us. We agreed to do this and Arnold, who was always ready for a challenge, wanted to go first.

We sat in the circle again and Arnold was blindfolded. Robbo said he would hold Arnold's hat while he had a go. Arnold, blindfolded, lifted the pick and as he started to bring it down in the rubber ring Robbo placed Arnold's hat on the rubber ring. The point of the pick went straight through Arnold's hat!

We all fell about laughing at the way Robbo had conned us and the look on Arnold's face when he tore off the blindfold and saw his hat on the pick blade had us in hysterics for days.

«««««««««««««»»»»»»»»»»»»»

Sometimes when I was a haulage lad, to make the time go quicker down the pit, we would devise games or make up limericks or verse. I made this masterpiece up, but could not understand why it was not appreciated:

(To the tune of 'Galway Bay')

If you ever go across the fields
From Mongeham
You will find there at the breaking
Of your day
You can sit and watch the moonlight
Over Eastry
And watch the sun go down
On Sandwich Bay

And if theres going to be
A life hereafter
And somehow I am sure
There's going to be
You can stand and watch
The Deal boatmen
Digging lugworm
And have some winkles
Found at Kingsdown
For your tea

«««««««««««««»»»»»»»»»»»»»

I think Knobby from Dover deserves a mention, he is a right Dover Shark.

If you studied Knobby closely he was not the hard bitten, straight talking character he liked to portray himself as. Sure enough he called a spade an **"effing shovel"** but when you got to know him he was as soft as the rest of us.

On one occasion my wife, Shirley, and I decided to go to Dover one Saturday night with the intention of having a couple of drinks, followed by a nice Chinese meal at the Good Luck Chinese restaurant.

We walked into the Park Inn in Ladywell by the Town Hall and a voice called out **"You can f**k off for a start!"**. My wife said **"Who on earth is that?!"**.

It was Knobby of course and after Knobby and I both introduced our wives to one another. My wife and I were treated to one of the best nights I have ever enjoyed in Dover and there have been quite a few over the years.

Knobby and his two mates at Betteshanger (the two Brians) were not exactly a law unto themselves, but when they were given a job to do, like a lot of other good pit men, liked to be left alone to get on with it.

There was, however, one overman at Betteshanger who was a stickler for wanting to know what was going on and when he was told on numerous occasions to **"eff off"** and what would happen if he did not, he had this saying **"You will have to get in the queue."**

This overman one day walked into the heading where Knobby and the two Brians were working and started to complain about bits of paper and other rubbish lying about and said **"Look at the state of this heading, it's a disgrace for Gods sake, throw all the rubbish on the conveyor belt."**

As one Knobby and the two Brians picked up the overman and threw him on the conveyor belt. As the overman disappeared towards the pit bottom, his voice came back **"I SUPPOSE YOU THINK THAT'S FUNNY KNOBBY!"**

«««««««««««««»»»»»»»»»»»»»

Whenever it came to making compensation claims, the Kent miners were never backwards in coming forward.

Before cap lamps were given to all underground workers, astigmos or 'eye stag' as miners preferred to call it, was one way of giving a chance to have time off and perhaps claim a bit of money from the pit bosses. Eye stag they claimed was very painful and left miners almost blind and unable to focus correctly.

One Kent miner put in a claim for this complaint and went to see an eye specialist who did not believe the miner was as bad as he made out, because the miner overdid it a bit by staggering into the room and blundered about as though he was completely blind.

The eye specialist guided the Kent miner to a chair and asked the miner to read the letters on a screen. **"What screen?"** said the Kent miner **"I can't see any screen."**

The eye specialist then said **"I am going to switch on different coloured lights and I want you to tell me what colour they are."**

"Okay pal" said the miner, so the eye specialist switched on different coloured lights and asked the miner what colour they were. The miner still made out he could see nothing.

The eye specialist thought **"Right I will give you an object you can see."** The eye specialist went outside the rear of his office and picked up a dustbin lid and went back into his office held the dustbin lid up in front of the miner and said **"What do you see?"**

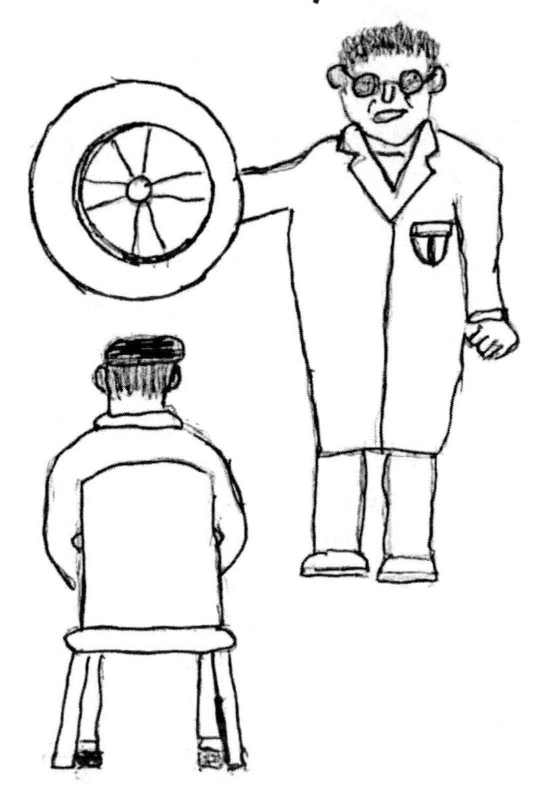

"Is it a threepenny bit?" asked the Kent miner.

«««««««««««««»»»»»»»»»»»»»

It is strange when you live in an area for years and perhaps a few streets away is someone you may never meet. The same can be said working in a big factory or coal mine. You can work there all your life and there will be people or workmates you will never meet. This was the reason two old miners clashed in the pit bottom one day.

Both of them were afflicted with a bad stutter and though this is a cross they have to bear, their workmates usually make it easier for them by pretending not to notice it.

The day this event occurred, both arrived in the pit bottom at the end of the shift and were stood near to one another, when someone started a conversation about something or other and one of the old lads who stuttered decided to give his opinions and the other old fellow said to the first chap **"Who who who do you th th think your your m m mocking?"**

The first stutterer replied **"And who who who do you you think y y your f f f**king mocking?!"**

At first the rest of the men stood there, they thought the two old men were messing about and doing their party piece but when the coats came off and punches started flying they got between the two old gladiators and it was then realised that in spite of them both working at Betteshanger for years their paths had never crossed before.

This event had to be reported and when they had to go before the manager I am sure he must have found it hard to keep a straight face.

«««««««««««««»»»»»»»»»»»»»

On the coalface the job of charge hand, Monkey Puff or Puffler was someone on the team who had been elected by the rest of the team to sort out any problems so that the rest of the team could get on with the work.

He could liaise with both union and management and with other charge hands on other coalfaces could stop the pit working if they were not satisfied with the situation. It is only fair to say that the majority of charge hands were level headed and wanted nothing more than to get on with the job and see that their team made a good wage.

I remember for a while on one coalface that I was working on nobody wanted to be the charge hand and only after a lot of persuasion one of the lads called Bob agreed to give it a try. Whenever a problem came up, such as no timber for the heading, or coalface, or perhaps a breakdown with some machinery, someone would get on the tannoy system and call **"Bob, so and so's happened what shall we do?"** Bob would probably be trying to sort out some other problem at the same time and you would hear his frustrated voice reply **"Oh f**k it!"**

He said this so often the rest of the team named him Bobby F**kitt!

When the colliers and heading men were on contract in the days before conveyor belts, they depended on having a constant supply of tubs so that they could get a good wage and bonus.

I have heard tales of chargehands coming to blows over who's coalface or heading was going to get the next run of tubs. Usually about Friday if the coalface had already made a good wage plus bonus the men on the coalface and headings could not care less who had the tubs.

One Friday morning two chargehands were stood at a junction looking at a run of eight empty tubs and one of the chargehands said to the other chargehand **"Go on you can have these tubs."**
The other chargehand said **"No you have them."**

For about a minute each chargehand tried to get the other chargehand to take the tubs. A Deputy stood there suggested that they have a wrestling match, the best of three falls gets the run of tubs.

"Bugger that!" said the first one **"I MIGHT WIN THE BLOODY THINGS!"**

««««««««««««««»»»»»»»»»»»»»»

Years ago if a coal face worker had an accident and was unable to work as a collier or ripper, he was given the chance of becoming a deputy or sholfirer depending on how experienced he was.

It was accepted that if he was a level headed guy and stood for no nonsense, he could take on the deputy's duties and swat up on the theory side of the job later.

One chap who had to give up coalface work became a deputy and was doing fine, but one day he noticed one of the main supply roadways to the coaling district had one or two bad bits of roof, where shale was falling through the timber behind the rings and landing on the rail track.

He decided it should be reported in case it derailed the mine cars with supplies. When he wrote his report at the end of the shift he thought it would be a good idea to suggest that sheets of corrugated iron behind the rings would solve the problem.

After years of hard work and getting out of the habit of reading and studying, his memory of spelling big words like, 'corrugated' was a bit vague. He was not sure how corrugated was spelt and did not want the other deputies to think he was thick, so he wrote sheets of **'crinkly tin'**.

When all coalfaces and headings used to be on individuals contracts, if your coalface or heading hit a problem that stopped them earning good money, they applied to the management to be put on a day wage until conditions allowed them to earn better money.

On one occasion a certain coalface at Betteshanger had run into problems and half of the team were sent to an area where there was a lot of spillage under the conveyor belt. They were told to clean it all up and throw it all on the conveyor belt.

When they arrived at the area to be cleaned there were no tools to do the work. They never bothered to get in touch with a deputy or overman and just sat around talking, and chewing tobacco.

All of a sudden an undermanager appeared and asked **"What did they think they were on their daddies yacht or something."**

The colliers said it was not their fault that there were no shovels.
The undermanager said **"Right I will get some shovels sent in for you."**
One of the colliers decided to act as spokesman and asked **"What do you want us to do in the meantime?"**

The undermanager managed to keep a straight face, and replied **"Lean on one another till then."**

««««««««««««««»»»»»»»»»»»»»»

Some of the most humorous comments I have heard in the mine are when the miners are either travelling into work or away from work.

One Monday morning in the seventies I was sat in the Paddy (Man Rider) with my work mates and I was kind of half listening to a couple of young colliers in the next compartment who were discussing the weekend just passed.
"Did you get yourself rigged out like you said you would on Friday?" asked the first young collier.

"Yeah" said the other young collier **"My mates and I went up to London on Saturday and we got all the latest gear."**
"What did you end up with?" asked the first young collier.
"I got one of those new style jackets with the sharp shoulders and narrow waists, a tailored shirt with ruffles on the front, a pair of flared trousers and a Kipper tie."

Two middle aged colliers, who like me, were ear-holing what was being said sat in the same compartment as me. One of them turned to the other, who came from the Midlands, and said **"What's a Kipper tie Brummie?"**

On reflection I don't think he could have asked a worse person, considering the way Brummies talk. Brummie, with a look of boredom on his face, answered **"It's what you drink with toast and butter!"**

«««««««««««««»»»»»»»»»»»»»

I only ever once saw Dick Sullivan look angry.

Dick like any other Welshman I knew loved to sing and at the drop of a hat would burst into song, so it was no surprise one Saturday night when Dick was at Betteshanger Club and there was a bit of a dance and sing song going on, that Dick without much encouragement went upon the stage to sing.

A favourite of Dicks at the time was **"That Lucky Old Sun"** and as Dick gave forth passionately with these words:

Up in the Morning
Out on the job
Work like the Devil
For my pay

Someone in the audience called out **"I don't know about you working like the Devil for your pay Dick, you've been on light work for the last ten years!"**

It was as I have said the only time I saw Dick look angry, but after a split second of annoyance, Dick the trouper that he was, just ignored the fool who was getting angry looks from the rest of the crowd and carried on with the rest of the song as only Dick could.

The mention of light work reminds me of a funny incident when I was a haulage lad.

Light work was jobs that were given to older miners who were beyond being able to work on coalfaces of ripping. Also to men who had been injured, or suffered with their chest.

I had this job taking haulage clips off a run of eight tubs and sending them on to the next stage of the journey where they were chained to a haulage rope and sent farther into the workings to be loaded with coal at the coal loading point.

On the day in question I happened to look towards the pit bottom and in the distance I saw four cap lamps being waved in all directions. I thought perhaps the haulage lads towards the pit bottom were sending me a message by bush telegraph.

The cap lamps were gradually getting nearer, so I called out to Jack, this old deputy who was standing in for our regular deputy 'Robbo', if he could make out what was going on.

Old Jack was as baffled as I was and it was only after the lights got to where we stood, which had overhead lighting, that we found out that it was four men who were on light work, who were oiling pulleys and rope return wheels.

I do not want anybody to think that I am making fun of their disabilities but in a way you can see what the humorous side of this is.

Of the four chaps in question, one suffered with back trouble and seemed to be bent forward from the hips. Another had very bad feet and his head and upper body bobbed from side to side. The other two limped badly with injuries to their legs. One with his left leg and the other with his right, so you can see why these cap lamps were bobbing about.

Jack the deputy looked at them and said **"Come on you old buggers, let's have a bit of rhythm on the job"** and to the tune of the 'Keel Row' started to chant **"Da da di da da di da da di da da"** which naturally I and the rest of the young haulage lads thought was funny.

Every time those old lads came by the junction where we worked we would do the chant and the four old chaps, I would like to add took it all in good part.

«««««««««««««»»»»»»»»»»»»»

A miner who lived in Margate was having a moan about the distance he had to travel each day to get to Betteshanger for work.

The reason he had to travel so far and get up so early in the morning was that he originally worked at Chislet, which closed in the late sixties, and like a lot of other ex-Chislet miners who lived in the Margate and Ramsgate area. He opted to work at Betteshanger after the closure of Chislet.

An old miner who's family had moved down from the North in the early thirties said **"That's nowt where I worked at a pit up Yorkshire as a young lad, I had to travel twice as far as that each day and cross two fields to get there."**

"You mean there was no road into the colliery and you had to cross two fields to get there?" said the miner from Margate.
"Oh aye" said the old Yorky **"There was a road into the colliery, but I had to cross Sheffield and Huddersfield!"**

««««««««««««««»»»»»»»»»»»»»

I once heard the NUM described as the guards regiment of the Trade Union movement. Out of all the miners in the country I would say that the Kent miners were the most militant of all.

So is it any wonder that the Kent miners children's version of the old nursery rhyme goes:

Hickory Dickory Dock
The Mouse ran up the Clock
The Clock Struck
And the Kent Miners
Came out in Sympathy!

««««««««««««««»»»»»»»»»»»»»

The Kent NUM, like most of the other unions, always had a sprinkling of communist sympathisers. Some of them could go over the top, but most of them were good union men who put their workmates safety first and fought for fairer wages for the work you did.

There was one communist sympathiser who I worked with on the haulage system who had a cracking sense of humour. This was Teddy and he always made a joke about everything - even his little speeches when he had a small audience would develop into a farce, because he could never keep a straight face.

One day someone asked Teddy if it was true that life in Russia under Joe Stalin was really so grim. Teddy was trying to dispel this opinion, but as usual his face broke into a big grin and he told us a joke which went like this.

In Russia under Stalin's regime every action or manner or speaking had to be kept to a minimum.
Russian boy meets Russian girl and says **"Vot is your name?"**
Russian girl replies **"Olga"**
Russian boy asked **"From where do you come?"**
Russian girl says **"Vladivostok"**
Russian boy gets impatient and says **"ENOUGH OF THIS FOURPLAY. LET'S HAVE SEX!"**

««««««««««««««»»»»»»»»»»»»»

Teddy always waved his hands about when he was talking (like Dennis Skinner or Tony Benn) and one guy told us that Teddy, like a lot of other self styled orators, would be speechless if he could not use his hands when he was talking and said he would prove it.

Later that shift when things were a bit slack and about half a dozen of us were stood in a group Teddy decided once more to try and convert us to communism.

Teddy's hands were flying all over the place and his mouth was going ten to the dozen and suddenly to prove his point the guy who told us about Teddy not being able to speak without using his hands, stepped forward and grabbed Teddy's hands and said **"Speak now Teddy!"**
Teddy was so taken aback and flustered he was speechless for about fifteen seconds and when he did manage to speak all he could say was **"boll**ks!"**

««««««««««««««»»»»»»»»»»»»»

At a union meeting one Sunday morning at Deal Welfare Club, the Chairman opened the meeting with a complaint about rumours that the union committee was handling the affaires of the NUM badly.

In the words of the Chairman, certain allegations had been made and he would like the **"Alligators"** to go through the normal channels with their complaints.

««««««««««««««»»»»»»»»»»»»»

I don't need to remind the lads who worked at Betteshanger how nice the meat pies were, that were made, and sold at the canteen there.

The ladies who worked there could never seem to make enough because they were so popular and it was quite a regular thing for some lads to take them home for their wives and children to try.

One day Lanc was a bit late getting to the canteen and asked the lady serving behind the counter for a cup of tea and a meat pie. The canteen lady told Lanc that there was only twelve pies left and she had strict orders to save them for a party of visitors who were on a visit down the mine and would be calling at the canteen.

Lanc said to the canteen lady **"If I was the gaffer and asked you for a meat pie, would you give me one?"**
"I suppose I would have to" replied the canteen lady.
"Well the gaffer's not coming" said Lanc **"So I'll have his!"**

««««««««««««»»»»»»»»»»»»

To go back to the time that I worked on the pit top with Jock repairing mine cars.

I remember an episode which looking back happened so quickly and for a couple of hours had the officials on the pit top running about like blue arsed flies trying to find the culprit.

What happened was that the No. 1 circuit by the pit shaft had just not long got underway after being rebuilt and the tannoy system had just been installed. It was not quite working right, so every now and then the control point at the offices would test the system and the Manager would call different parts of the pit and ask them if they were hearing him loud and clear.

I was working on a mine car near one of these tannoy boxes when along came this lad called Jeff, who was not the full shilling and who was usually given menial jobs to do and acted as Chief Gofer. For no apparent reason Jeff walked up to the tannoy box while the Manager was speaking, pressed the speak button and said **"F**k off you bastard!"**

All hell broke loose. The manager blew his top and said over the tannoy **"IF I FIND OUT WHO SAID THAT I WILL SACK HIM IMMEDIATELY!"**

We were all questioned by pit top foremen to see who had swore at the Manager but we could not drop Jeff in it and Jeff had enough between his ears to realise what he had done and made himself scarce for a long while after that!

««««««««««««»»»»»»»»»»»»

Jeff needed a bit of extra cash, because he could not get any overtime at the pit, so he decided to go and get a Saturday job at the Deal Market.
He approached the owner of the fruit and veg stall and asked him of he wanted an assistant. The owner of the stall decided to give Jeff a try and said "okay". A customer approached and the stall owner said to Jeff "Serve this gentleman."

The customer said to Jeff **"Are these apples ripe?"**
"I don't know" said Jeff.
"How much do they cost?" asked the customer.
"I don't know" said Jeff.
"Some use you are!" said the customer, and walked away.

The stall owner said to Jeff **"Let me serve the next customer, and just follow what I say"**
Another customer came up to the stall, and like the one before asked **"Are these apples ripe?"**
The stall owner said **"Some are and some are not"**
"How much do they cost?" asked the customer.

"Fourpence a pound" said the stall owner.
"I think I will buy some" said the customer.
"If you don't, someone else will" replied the stall owner cheerfully.

After serving the customer, the stall owner turned to Jeff, and said **"That's all there is to it: 'some are and some are not', they're fourpence a pound, 'if you don't someone else will'."**

"I think I've got it" said Jeff.

A man approached Jeff at the stall and asked him **"Could you tell me how to get to Alfred Square?"**
"Some are and some are not" said Jeff.
"Are you trying to be funny?" asked the man.
"Fourpence a pound" said Jeff.
"I've a good mind to punch you on the nose!" exclaimed the man.
"IF YOU DON'T, SOMEONE ELSE WILL!" said Jeff.

««««««««««««»»»»»»»»»»»

Officials, love them or loathe them, they were necessary. They were there to check for gas and many other jobs, so that the other underground workers could get on with the jobs in hand. Most of them were ex coalface workers or rippers (heading men) and knew the score and with a little understanding for certain problems, knew when to show their faces and when to leave well alone.

In my experience I can think of many officials who the lads would do anything for and others who had a habit of rubbing the lads up the wrong way. One under-manager who seemed to have everyone's respect was Sam. Sam was no pushover, but if you reached the target for output, Sam always turned up on the spot and congratulated the team in question.

This gives me an excuse to bring Sam into my story. I would also like to mention 'Benny'. The scene is set on '22' coalface at Betteshanger, where Benny was helping out by coming off the coalface to man the switches in the main gate (loading point).

Sam was at the other end of the coalface about to bring a party of nurses through the coalface on a visit. Sam's voice came over the tannoy system **"Watch your language lads, I have got a party of young ladies coming through."**

About ten minutes later when Sam and the nurses must have been about halfway through the coalface, someone called over the tannoy **"What time is it Benny?"** Benny not thinking called back **"My name is 'Little Ben' not f**king Big Ben!"**
Sam's disappointed voice sounded over the tannoy **"Benny what have I just asked you?"**
When the nurses came off the coalface a red faced Benny apologised to a smiling bunch of nurses who assured Benny they had heard a lot worse in their time.

««««««««««««»»»»»»»»»»»»

One undermanager who knew how to treat the lads was nicknamed 'Bonny Lad'.

He got this nickname because coming from Geordie Land he would always greet you with 'Hallo bonny Lad'. 'The Bonny Lad' was a crafty old sod, because he would always turn up where a gang of men would be working just before snaptime and by just looking could tell if things were alright.

Then he would chat to the lads and looking at someone's snap tin would say **"That's a bonny piece of cake you have there son, did your mother make it?"**
The lad in question would feel obliged to offer the Bonny Lad a bit which was always accepted. He would always say what a grand job you were all doing and he would be showered with offers of chocolate biscuits, buns and numerous half cups of tea and coffee. If ever there

was a case for the carrot beating the stick the 'Bonny Lad' and 'Sam' were prime examples.

«««««««««««««»»»»»»»»»»»»»

When I was working on the West Development at Betteshanger in the seventies there was a deputy called Fred who lived in Ramsgate.

Fred was born in Wales but claimed he was a Ramsgate Redneck because he had lived in Ramsgate since he was a youngster. Fred had a nice nature and boy did he need it with the lads he had working under him. They were always playing jokes on one another and Fred had his share of it.

Fred started walking about the district with a deputies walking stick and some of the lads targeted Fred for a practical joke. When Fred went into a heading to fire the explosives he would leave his deputies stick well back from where the detonating battery was.

The lads decided that while Fred was doing a safety check before firing they would each day saw off an inch of his deputies stick and see how long it was before he twigged it.

This actually went on for four days before Fred realised what had happened and I don't think the lads would have laughed so much if they knew what Fred called them in Welsh!

On another occasion something got in my eye and it was really painful.

I said to Fred that I would have to go out of the pit to get it seen to because it was driving me mad. Fred told me to go and get my plastic water bottle, which I did, and sitting me down on a tool box, he took a big swig from my water bottle, swilled it about and spat it out.

Then he took another mouthful and leaned over me and held my eyelids apart, and before I realised what he intended to do he gently spat in my eye.

Guess what, it did the trick. If it had not, I probably would have decked him!

««««««««««««««»»»»»»»»»»»»»

No two persons are exactly the same, or think the same. Which I suppose is a good thing.

FV or 'Vom' as he was called for short took some working out. He totally confused his mates one day when he told them about an altercation or bust up he had had with his wife.

Vom was on the night shift but did not feel too well and did not fancy the thought of going to work that night.

As anyone who has worked on a night shift knows, you have to be mentally capable as well as physically capable, for it takes a strong character to be going to work when it seems everybody else is relaxing and watching the telly, or having a night at your local pub.

Anyway Vom informed his wife (who tended to wear the trousers) that he felt ill and no way could he face going to the pit that night. His wife blew her top and the pair of them had a right ding dong.

Up to that point Vom held his nerve. A case of a worm turning. She could see he was not well, but was also determined not to go to work that night. She was equally determined to keep poor old Vom down trodden and said to Vom **"If you are not going to work go and fill the coal bucket for the morning."**

Instead of consolidating his new won ground, Vom went outside and started filling the coal bucket. His wife suddenly appeared at the door, threw his coat and snap tin out, slammed the door and shouted **"Now bugger off to work!"**

Any miner worth his salt would have kicked down the door and put her in her place, but not Vom. He crawled off to work as ill as he felt.

When relating all this to his mates a few weeks later, they all said what their reaction would have been. Vom winked at them and said **"I got my own back on her."**

"How was that?" they asked.

A big smile spread across his face and he told them **"I stopped on an hours overtime at the end of the shift."**

Like his mates I am still trying to work that one out...

«««««««««««««»»»»»»»»»»»»»

As with most jobs the guys bring things in from home to show their mates and the miners are no different, but one lad used to bring all the latest girlie magazines. You name it, he brought it. It must have cost him a small fortune, because they are not cheap (don't ask me how I know).

The girlie mags were usually passed along the coal face and headings for perusal and every now and then this lad would collect them together and take them home again (probably to add to his huge collection). After being handled by all the colliers and rippers, I should think the mags were hardly recognisable. Especially the naughty bits.

One pile he had ready to take home, he strapped to the pillion of his motorbike one very windy day and set off from the pithead baths at Betteshanger to Deal.

He got as far as Sholden when all the girlie mags flew off the pillion. He stopped the motorbike and started running round trying to collect his precious girlie mags whenever the traffic would allow.

Just then a bus full of miners from Betteshanger stopped to let one of the lads off who lived at Sholden. When they saw what was going on the whole bus started cheering. The girlie mag fan just carried on collecting his precious books and did not seem to care about anything else.

For about a week after that, it was the topic of conversation. If that had been me I would have died of shame or left the area for good, but this lad did not bat an eyelid!

««««««««««««»»»»»»»»»»»»

In later years the name timber lad was changed to Supply Worker and one young lad who was on supplies was 'Dixon'.

He was a lovely lad and a good worker and if he had any faults the only two I could think of was he was always hungry and would eat all his snap or sandwiches going into work and when it came to snaptime he had nothing to eat and would go around asking if anyone had got any sandwiches, cakes or biscuits they did not want.

No matter how much he cadged and that was always quite a bit, he still seemed hungry. The only other fault he had, if you could call it a fault, was that at the end of the shift as soon as his backside rested on the paddy or manrider to be taken out to the pit bottom he would fall asleep.

When the paddy reached the point where you disembarked for the pit bottom most men and lads would jump off the paddy and charge to the pit bottom hoping to get on the first ride up the pit shaft.

Whoever sat with Dixon on the paddy would usually awaken Dixon when the paddy neared the pit bottom and say 'Pit bottom Dixon' and Dixon would jump off the paddy and charge towards the pit bottom and God help anyone who got in his way.

But one day the paddy was on its way out to the pit bottom and as usual Dixon had nodded off. When the paddy reached another pick up point called 60's, where men from another district got on the paddy one of the lads sat next to Dixon woke him and said 'Pit bottom Dixon'.

Dixon jumped off the paddy and set off for the pit bottom like 'Red Rum' or 'Desert Orchid'. 60's was a good half mile away from the pit bottom and it was not 'til Dixon reached an empty pit bottom that he realised something was not quite right.

For a long time after that when the paddy neared 60's we would all shout **"PIT BOTTOM DIXON!"**

J.BRANNAN
'84
©

DOWN THE PUB AND UP THE CLUB

The Kent Miners enjoyed a pint down the pub as much as the next man. It wasn't just the pleasant effects of the alcohol after a hard day at work, but also a great place for socialising with workmates. Along with Deal's notorious pubs, The Miners Welfare Clubs were (and still are) great hubs of activity and banter.

««««««««««««»»»»»»»»»»»»

I remember being a young teenager living in Betteshanger village in the late forties. My mates and I would be allowed to go in the Betteshanger club and if we behaved ourselves we were allowed to play darts and rummy with cards. We would listen to our dads and their friends telling stories about their experiences in the first world war.

The story that I thought took some beating was a bloke called Jack who was a young private in the Lancashire regiment. He was in the first retreat from Mons and was running so fast he caught up with a hare in full flight running the same way. He said he gave it a kick up the arse and said to it **"GET OUT THE WAY AND LET SOME OTHER BUGGER RUN THAT CAN RUN!"**

««««««««««««»»»»»»»»»»»»

When the mines were nationalised in 1947, it was decided that there should be some kind of celebration. One such event was a dinner to get to know the chairman of the Kent Coalfield, who had been appointed by the Government.

The person they appointed was an ex navy man called Admiral Woodhouse, this amazed most of the mining community in spite of him saying **"I don't know anything about coalmining but I am willing to learn."**

Anyway to get back to the PR as they call it these days. It was decided to have a dinner in the Welfare Club at Mill Hill. There was still a certain amount of rationing on, because of the second World War, and the menu put before the NCB officials, pit managers and union members was anything but sumptuous. It consisted of a thin slice of ham, a couple of boiled potatoes and a bit of salad.

After the usual speeches the Admiral who was the guest of honour did not seem to be hungry and was pushing the bit of ham around is plate. This was noticed by an old miner about twenty feet away, who called out **"HEY ADMIRAL. IF THA DON'T WANT THAT HAM CHUCK THE BUGGER UP HERE!"**

«««««««««««««»»»»»»»»»»»»»

Little Billy hardly topped five foot but what he lacked in stature, he made up for in a loud Yorkshire voice, plus bravado. I remember someone in the pit bottom once listening to Billy threatening what he was going to do to someone, remarking **"If you were stood round the corner and heard Billy but could not see him, you would think Billy was seven feet tall and built like the Incredible Hulk."**

Billy had a nasty habit of listening in to someone's conversation and butting in and after being told to mind his own business would start to take off his coat and challenge them to a fight.

Most people would ignore him but on one occasion he was earholing someone's conversation in the Welfare Club and as usual butted in and after being told to keep his nose out and go away, Billy started throwing punches at the man who stood at least six feet tall.

The other fellow grabbed Billy by the front of his jacket and held Billy at arms length and carried on with his conversation. Meanwhile Billy was still throwing punches which were falling short by at least six inches.

After a couple of minutes the tall man looked around the bar and said **"Does anyone own this?"** indicating Billy who was still trying to connect with his fists.

I suppose we should feel a bit sorry for Billy because try as he may to be recognised as one of the lads he always seemed to be a victim of a putdown. Once he was attending a union meeting at the Welfare Club on a Sunday morning and as the heated discussion was reaching a crescendo, Billy got up to say his piece but seemed to be ignored by the Union Committee. Billy shouted **"Mr Chairman I am on my feet"** and some wag at the back of the hall shouted **"Well stand up then!"**

Off came Billy's coat and the usual challenge to step outside and fight!

««««««««««««»»»»»»»»»»»

One annual holiday in the fifties, a gang of us young lads, who worked at the pits, were in a pub in Deal and we were at a bit of a loose end at what we could do to amuse ourselves. A couple of lads there owned cars of some description; someone suggested that we all pile into the cars and visit the Five Bells in Ringwould.

On arriving at the Five Bells, no doubt, the landlord was glad of our custom, but he looked a bit irritated. One of the locals asked him what the matter was. The landlord said **"Have a look in the saloon bar."** The local chap stuck his head through to the saloon bar, turned back and said **"See what you mean!"**

We of course were dying to know what was going on in the saloon bar, so a couple of our crowd took a peek. Their faces lit up with smiles and one of them said **"Hey lets go in the saloon bar, you'll enjoy this."**

We all trooped into the saloon bar and guess who was the source of the landlords' irritation. None other than Lanc! Lanc had the shooting rights on some property over the back of Ringwould and it had been a good day for Lanc, if not for the landlord of the Five Bells. There were about ten dead rabbits lying on the tables of the saloon bar and Lanc was trying to get the customers in there to take them home with them.

One couple who we understood were on holiday in Deal had the misfortune to call in the Five Bells for a drink and Lanc had parked himself on them, insisting that they take two of the dead rabbits when they went and Lanc would not take no for an answer. It was only when Lanc recognised our lot that he left them much to the couple's relief, because the woman looked as though she was going to be sick any minute.

The couple saw their chance and decided to nip out and get in their car while Lanc had his back turned talking to us. They had almost made it to the car when Lanc turned round and said **"Hey up! They have left their rabbits behind!"** and grabbed the two rabbits off the table. In spite of having had a good drink, he nipped smartly out the door and just as the woman was about to get into the car, said **"Here you are luv, you forgot your rabbits!"**

The poor woman took the rabbits off Lanc and put them on the floor of their car and away they went. We all felt Lanc had gone a bit over the top with his generosity, but our turn was yet to come. We had decided to move on to somewhere else and Lanc insisted that we took all of the dead rabbits with us.

With our best suits and ties on, which was the drill when you went out in those days, we did not want to be squashed into a couple of cars with loads of dead rabbits, but to humour Lanc we set off towards Ripple and every hundred yards or so we stopped and threw a dead rabbit out of the car and over the hedge or in a field. I expect the couple on holiday did the same!

««««««««««««»»»»»»»»»»»»

There was this chap called Steve who was what we called a shaftsman. They had to inspect the two pit shafts every day and do any maintenance that was needed.

Steve worked on regular afternoons 2pm 'til 10pm. He would always dash through the Pit Head baths at the end of the shift and get to the Betteshanger Club where the steward would have two pints of beer on the counter so Steve could drink them in the drinking up time. The reason for this was the steward had to close the bar at 10pm in those days, but there was always fifteen minutes allowed for people to finish their drinks.

One bitterly cold night Steve dashed in half frozen and grabbed his first pint and knocked it back in one go, which was his usual practice, and passed out spluttering and gasping for breath. The other customers did not know what to do and Grandad B who was having a drink with my dad at the time said **"Slit his throat and let some air in."**

My dad said **"Don't talk so bloody silly"** and my grandad said **"Why not? That's what they do to racehorses!"**

Steve, I'm glad to say, after an anxious five minutes coughed loudly and started breathing normal again, took his second pint to one of the tables and carried on drinking.

««««««««««««»»»»»»»»»»»»

Ernie worked at Betteshanger before he became a landlord and being a Yorkshire man stood no nonsense, but always gave you value for your money when you drank at his pub, because he always had a joke or funny tale to tell you.

I was in his pub the Brickmakers Arms one day and he was sniffing and sneezing, coughing and spluttering. He should have been in bed, not stood behind the bar, but Ernie being a tough tyke decided to fight it.

"That's a right cold you've got there Ernie" I said.
"Aye yer right there kid I'm snottier than Rotherham bobby!" he replied.

Ernie's wife, (the long suffering 'Ada') told us once about a day out Ernie had with a lot of other pub landlords, who referred to themselves as the 'Licentious Victuallers' and usually the day started with a trip to one of the breweries and the landlords always made the most of the free drink available.

On the day Ada told us about, she was just retiring to bed after a busy day and evening holding the fort, when she thought she could hear someone singing outside. She realised it was Ernie walking down Park Avenue towards the Brickmakers Pub serenading the Victoria Park community after enjoying a great day out.

Top of the hit parade at that time was the great Jim Reeves song 'I love you because' and just as Ernie finished the bit **"no matter what the world may say about me"**, Ada, who had opened the bedroom window, shouted up the street to Ernie **"IT'S WHAT THE NEIGHBOURS WILL SAY THAT I AM WORRIED ABOUT!"**

««««««««««««»»»»»»»»»»»

Don was a little chap who came down from London and if he was not born within the sound of Bowbells, he had all the chat of a 'Cor blimey'. He was burning the candle at both ends, because he was working down the pit on night shift and working on delivering coal from the pit top during the day.

Mister Leivers who had just become manager of Betteshanger was just about settled into the job and decided one Saturday night to pop into the Admiral Keppel pub at Upper Deal for a drink. Don also decided he had earned a good drink, also popped into the Keppel and being a chatty sort decided to go over and talk to this bloke sitting on his own.

Introducing himself, as was Don's happy go lucky attitude, he soon got chatting away to the stranger ten to the dozen. After a while the stranger asked Don what he did for a living. Don gave the stranger a sly wink and told him that in his opinion he had got it made.

The stranger was starting to warm to this likeable Londoner and asked him what he meant. **"Well"** said Don **"I work at Betteshanger Colliery on the night shift and after having a shower, and some breakfast in the canteen, I do a couple of days a week delivering household coal from the pit top."**

On the following Monday night when Don reported for work for the night shift, Don had a note on his lamp to report to the manager the following day. Don reported to the offices on the pit top the following day and was ushered into the managers office and imagine his shock when he saw that the man sitting there was Mr Leivers, the man he had been chatting to on Saturday night in the Admiral Keppel.

Mr Leivers gave Don the ultimatum, work nights at Betteshanger, or work on the coal lorries. Don chose the night shift.

««««««««««««««»»»»»»»»»»»»»

The Kent miners had been on strike for two weeks and a group of them were sat at their local club making their pint of beer last as long as possible. The door of the public bar opened and one of their mates came in and ordered a pint of beer. When the barman served him, he looked at his mates sat with about an inch of beer in their pint pots.

He lifted up his pint and knocked it back with one gulp, and then said **"Are you lads having another one?"** They couldn't believe their luck and picked up their pint pots and said **"Cheers, I don't mind if I do"** and finished off what was left in their glasses.

"Lucky bastards" said the bloke at the bar **"I CAN'T AFFORD ANOTHER ONE MYSELF!"** and with that beat a hasty retreat, followed by choice words about his pedigree from other drinkers there.

««««««««««««»»»»»»»»»»»»

This chap Bert had been having a good drink at the Welfare Club in Mill Hill one night and was making his way home down Arthur Road when he was suddenly taken short and knew he would never make it to where he lived in Davis Avenue so he nipped into a garden in Arthur Road and dropped his pants and relieved himself.

When he was finished he stood up and being as it was a bright moonlit night he turned round to look at what he had done and was amazed to find there was nothing to be seen. No crap, nothing. **"I can't believe this"** he said to himself.

He went on his way but that night he could not sleep, baffled at why there was nothing to be seen when he definitely knew he had relieved himself in that front garden. The following day he decided he would walk past the garden again and glance over the hedge and see if he could spot anything there.

Bert retraced his steps up Arthur Road and when he reached the garden in question the tenant of the house was stood in the garden and Bert sneaked a quick glance over the lawn and just to be sociable remarked to the chap stood there **"I must say you keep your garden nice."**

"Aye" replied the other chap **"BUT IT MAKES YOU WONDER IF IT IS ALL WORTHWHILE WHEN SOME BUGGER GOES AND S**TS ON YOUR TORTOISE!"**

««««««««««««»»»»»»»»»»»»

Do you know what a lake is, or to lake?

To lake in a lot of mining areas means to have a shift off. There is also an expression called 'Colliers Monday'. This is where miners who have had a good booze up at the weekend cannot face the thought of going to work, so have a shift off and go to the pub or club to have some hair of the dog that bit them.

One Monday, a week before the annual three weeks holiday, a crowd of miners were sat in the Welfare Club in Mill Hill drinking steadily, when a young miner came in and ordered a drink at the bar. After the barman served him he asked the young fellow if he was going anywhere for his holiday.

The young miner replied that he was taking his wife and two kids to the Lake District. The barman could not resist such an opportunity and looking round at the crowd of drinkers said **"I THINK YOU ARE ALREADY THERE SON!"**

««««««««««««»»»»»»»»»»»

The next tale takes a bit of believing, but many of the old miners who worked at Betteshanger reckon it's true.

There were two miners who worked at Betteshanger who suffered with the same complaint. The complaint in question, I do not know the proper medical term, but we knew it as Wry Neck. It is where the head stays permanently on one side.

The two men are Alf and Joe, Alf's head was tilted to the left and Joe's head was tilted to the right, or vice versa. Joe always used the pit bus to get to work whilst Alf always used his motorbike.

One day Joe came out of the pit head baths and decided to nip over to the Betteshanger Social Club for a quick pint before catching the pit bus back to Deal. Joe stayed a bit too long at the club and when he got to the pit head baths, the last pit bus had gone. He was wondering what to do, when along came Alf on his motorbike. Alf realised Joe had missed the bus, so he stopped and told Joe to get on the pillion.

They set off for Deal and Alf called back to Joe **"Where shall I drop you off Joe?"**
"Anywhere in Deal will do" replied Joe.

They eventually rode down Queen Street and arrived at the only traffic lights in Deal at that time, and they were out of order. One of the local policemen was directing the traffic, because traffic also used the High Street in those days.

Alf stopped his motorbike while the policeman let some traffic along the High Street and when the policeman turned to look at Alf and Joe sat on the motorbike with Alf's head on one side and Joe's head on the other side, he said **"Come on you buggers make your minds up!"**

Joe heard about an operation that might cure his wry neck, so he consulted his doctor about it and his doctor told Joe that this operation was hit or miss but if Joe wanted to try it, he (the doctor) would put Joe's name forward for it.

This was done, and Joe was duly operated on and it was a success. When all the bandages were taken off, Joe was so pleased with the result he decided to go to the Deal Welfare Club and celebrate.
Joe walked into the bar and ordered a double whisky, and forgetting about his neck being straightened, threw the double whisky over his right shoulder!

««««««««««««««»»»»»»»»»»»»»

I have always had a deep respect for the Salvation Army. Besides the good work they do for the under privileged, when I served in the army in the early fifties most camps I was stationed at had an SA canteen and you could always get a good cheap meal there. After the uninspiring rubbish served in the cookhouse, the meals in the SA canteens were very popular and when you were skint, if you went along to the SA canteen you could always get a free cup of tea or cocoa and a bun.

I never pass the Salvation Army in the street without putting my hand in my pocket and dropping something in the tin. I have given up smoking for over ten years now and if I could give up the drink and swearing I would consider joining them!

The reason I mention the Salvation Army is that I recall a story that was passed down over the years. I would like to stress that no way do I intend to demean the Salvation Army. The story goes like this.

One Saturday night at chuck out time the Salvation Army band were playing outside the Mill Inn pub in Mill Hill. The miners and their wives and friends were on their way home from the Miners Welfare Club and the Mill Inn and formed a crowd around the band and some of them joined in the singing.

When the band stopped playing the major in charge held his hands up and said **"Brothers and sisters I would like you to listen to a few words from Brother William."**

A figure the miners knew well stepped forward. He was a miner who worked at Betteshanger who used to be an alcoholic. **"I used to be like you brothers and sisters, smoking, drinking and swearing, but now I have seen the light and now I an full of Salvation"** he said.

The major looked at him proudly and said **"Tell them again Brother William."**Perhaps it was the looks of disbelief on the faces of his workmates or the wry smiles that prompted Brother William to shout **"F**K THEM, I'VE ALREADY TOLD THEM ONCE!"**

BRANNAN
84

LEISURE PURSUITS

The miners set up rugby and football teams in East Kent, and frequent trips were made to see top division clubs around the country - allegiances often traced back to the towns the Kent miners and their families had originally come from. In addition, Deal's close proximity to the continent meant that trips to France were often arranged. But sometimes the best times could be had in Deal.

««««««««««««»»»»»»»»»»»

Over the years Betteshanger Rugby team and some of the lads who played for Betteshanger made quite a name for themselves as real tough guys. Dick Sullivan told me about one such guy who used to put the fear of God in the teams who played against Betteshanger, but eventually even he came off second best one day and ended up with a dislocated shoulder.

He was taken to Buckland Hospital at Dover where a doctor was doing his best to reset the shoulder and our rugby hero was shouting and hollering with pain. The matron of the hospital who was attending the birth of triplets at the maternity ward a good hundred yards away came to see what all the noise was about and when she saw the rugby player she said **"Stop this silly noise at once, There's a women in the maternity ward who has just had triplets and she did not make a quarter of the noise that you are making."**
"Yeah?" said the rugby player **"WELL TRY PUTTING ONE OF THEM BACK IN AND SEE WHAT SHE SAYS!"**

««««««««««««»»»»»»»»»»»

Dai and Yanto (I believe it's spelt Ianto) were very keen rugby fans and would go and watch Betteshanger rugby team at the Welfare Ground at Mill Hill. For a while Dai stopped going to watch the rugby matches and Yanto wondered why. One day Yanto met Dai in the street and asked Dai why he no longer went to watch the rugby at the Welfare Ground.

"Well Yanto it's like this boyo" said Dai **"The missus' keeps grabbing me to take her shopping every Saturday afternoon"**

"Dai, I never thought you of all people would let your wife stop you from watching the rugby" said Yanto.

"Well you know how it is" replied Dai **"Christmas is coming up and she wanted a hand to carry the extra shopping."**

"Look" said Yanto, who ruled the roost in his household, **"You come to the rugby on Saturday, and tell you missus, bugger the shopping!"**

"Righto Yanto" said Dai **"I'll see you at the Welfare Ground on Saturday."**

Saturday came and Yanto went to watch the rugby but Dai never turned up again.

"Wait till I see that down trodden wimp!" said Yanto to himself.

The following Monday morning, Yanto met Dai waiting for the pit bus to go to work and said **"What's the excuse this time Dai?"**

"Oh, I had every intention of watching the rugby" said Dai **"I was getting ready to go to the rugby and the missus said 'where do you think your going Dai?' I said to her, 'I'm going to the Welfare Ground to watch the rugby with Yanto'"**

"Oh no you are not! You are taking me shopping! she said. I said to her bugger the shopping, I'm going to the rugby. She could see I was determined to go and watch the rugby, so she lifted her skirt up to her waist and said Dai, you take me shopping and I will give you the best night of sex since the first night of our honeymoon."

"Well...I thought to myself, if it was a cracking game like playing Snowdown Colliery I would have been there. But seeing as it was only Folkestone, I thought fk it!"**

««««««««««««»»»»»»»»»»»»

Jeff had been invited by some lads who worked at Betteshanger to go with them and see a football match in London.

He was stood on Deal railway station and the train had arrived and Jeff looked at the train driver who was leaning out of his cab and asked **"Does this train stop at Charing Cross?"**

"I hope so" said the cockney driver **"If it don't it will wreck the bleeding station!"**

«««««««««««««»»»»»»»»»»»»»

Robbo played at centre forward for Betteshanger's football team, the equivalent of striker these days and was big and strong and could move very quick for a man of his size. He scored quite a few goals while playing for Betteshanger and in a way had a kind of fan club. Many a time when watching Betteshanger play on the Welfare ground at Mill Hill you could hear shouts of **"Give the ball to Robbo!"**

One day Betteshanger were awarded a penalty and the shout went up again **"Give it to Robbo, let Robbo take it!"** Robbo was given the honour of taking it. He placed the ball on the spot, walked back, ran up to take it and ballooned it over the crossbar. One cynical Betteshanger fan said **"ROBBO WANTS F**KING!"** He was immediately set upon by half a dozen women brandishing umbrellas!

«««««««««««««»»»»»»»»»»»»»

Coal miners are no different from any other workers when it comes to talking shop in their leisure time, but there are limits and places where it should not be discussed. I would like to give you an instance where my younger brother Jim and my cousin Bill and myself were stopped dead in our tracks outside the Tottenham Hotspur football ground one Saturday afternoon.

Jim and Bill were part of a heading team that was developing a coalface at Betteshanger and on the day in question we were on a day trip to London to watch a game of football between Spurs and

Burnley who were both top teams at that time in the old first division Circa 1961.

We were making our way along White Hart Lane to the end of a very long queue who were waiting to get into the ground when a voice called out **"Hey up we set two rings last night."** (Roof supports)
As I have said we were stopped dead in our tracks. Who would expect eighty miles away from where you lived and worked someone would shout about the progress of your workplace. It was of course a miner who worked on one of the other shifts from Jim and Bill.

The three of us all looked at one another and in perfect unison said **"OH FOR F**KS SAKE!"**

««««««««««««»»»»»»»»»»»»

This young miner who originally came from near Rotherham, was a devout Leeds United fan and whenever Leeds United played one of the London clubs he would set off from his home in Deal and make his way to London and meet some of his old mates and relations from Yorkshire who would travel down to watch the team play.

On one occasion after he had a few drinks with his old mates and relations said goodbye to them and made his way to Charing Cross station. He had an hour or so to wait for the next train back to Deal, so decided to go and have another pint to pass the time.

He noticed a pub near the station which belonged to the brewery called 'Friary Meux'. On entering the saloon bar, the only other person there was a rather prim looking young barmaid. Looking at what was on offer, he said to the sour faced barmaid **"I'll have a pint of Friary Meux best bitter please luv."**

When he said it he pronounced Meux as Mewks. The barmaid totally ignored him, so he repeated the order. She looked down her nose at him and replied **"Meux is pronounced Mews, the X is silent."**

"Are you going to serve me or what?" asked the young miner.

She finally served him, so the young miner sat down at a table and had his drink. 'The sooner I get out of here the better' thought the young miner, so he gulped down his pint of bitter and headed for the door.
Perhaps the barmaid felt a bit embarrassed at the way she had treated the young miner and said **"Goodnight sir."**
The young miner turned at the door and replied **"Bollo."**
"I beg your pardon sir?" enquired the snotty barmaid.
The young miner called back **"THE 'X' IS SILENT!"**

««««««««««««»»»»»»»»»»»»

Wilf, who came from Grimethorpe, and myself used to have a game or two of golf at Deal and we would swap jokes and generally put the world to rights.

What I admired about Wilf was that for all the years he had lived in this part of the country, he still talks like he came from Yorkshire yesterday. Anyway, why should he try and talk like us Cherrypickers?

One summers evening we had been playing golf and as we were driving along College Road where he lived, I said **"Where can I drop you off Wilf?"** He replied **"By ginnel yonder."**
"What the bloody hell is a ginnel?" I asked.
"Tha knows, bloody alleyway" said Wilf.

No wonder when foreigners learn perfect English and come to this country yet still cannot understand what we are saying, they must wonder if it has been worthwhile.

««««««««««««»»»»»»»»»»»»

Like most other occupations and professions, the families and relations pick up the jargon and slang used by their fathers and brothers who work in certain jobs.

One word I would like to mention concerning the mining industry is the word 'Spragg'.

Any miner who has gone through the process of haulage lad, timber lad and eventually coalface worker, will know that a spragg is a piece of wood anywhere between two to four feet long, that can be wedged between a rail sleeper and the front of a mine car or tub to stop it running away. The story I am about to tell happened on the sands of Ramsgate one summer.

A miner and his wife and children were spending one day of their annual holiday on the Ramsgate sands, when their youngest child who was about four years old asked his mother if he could have a ride on the donkeys.

The miner's wife was only too glad to give the young tot a treat, so she took him over to where the other mum's were sitting their children on the donkeys, getting ready for the next ride.

Plonking her son on one of the donkeys, she stood back and looking down she was aware of something coming from between the donkeys back legs and it was sticking in the sand.

She turned to the owner of the donkeys and said **"KICK THE SPRAGG OUT MISTER WE ARE READY TO GO!"**

«««««««««««««»»»»»»»»»»»»

Many old miners will remember the housing manager. His job was to allocate the houses belonging to the mining company and later the Coal Board to the miners and their families, and after that collect rent and see that the properties were looked after.

Miners as a rule were not known to have green fingers. After a hard days work down the mine the last thing on their minds was gardening. One day the housing manager was doing his rent collection round the circle at Betteshanger, when he noticed one garden covered in weeds and started to chastise the tenant about the state of the garden.

"Hang on pal" said the tenant **'If they are weeds, I'm going to sue Woolworths, it said on the packet, they were Marigolds!"**

«««««««««««««»»»»»»»»»»»»»

There was this old retired Kent miner and his wife who never seemed to do anything different, so his son, who was a pit deputy and his wife, decided to get the old chap and his wife out of their rut and treat them to the deputies and overman's annual dinner and dance.

This was appreciated by the old couple and on the night in question, they arrived at the venue. They were made welcome and met a lot of old friends that they had not seen for ages. Their son and his wife were used to these do's, but the old lad felt a bit embarrassed having to keep asking his son what knife or spoon to use.

Eventually the meal was over and the waiters and waitresses came round to serve the coffee. A waitress approached the old miner with a pot of coffee in one hand and a jug of hot milk in the other.

"Would you like black or white coffee sir?" she asked the old lad.

The old fellow had noticed the younger people showing off a bit and asking for black coffee, so he thought he'd try black coffee as it seems to be the 'in thing'.

"I'll have the black coffee, my luv" he told the pretty, young waitress, but not sure what he was going to get. The waitress poured the black coffee into his cup and went to move onto the next diner.

The old miner looked at the black coffee in his cup and said **"DON'T FORGET THE MILK, MY LUV!"**

«««««««««««««»»»»»»»»»»»»»

Sometimes when you hear a name or a word it conjures up in your mind your own picture.

The word 'Round House' was one such name that intrigued me. The 'Round House' in question was the turning to St Margarets Bay from the Deal Dover Road. In years gone by if you were sat on a bus going from Deal to Dover, when you got to this point the driver or conductor would call out **"Round House!"**

There was no round house or any other shape of a house to be seen, so one day as a young lad working down the pit I and my workmates were having our snap time break and for the sake of starting a conversation I asked if anyone knew why that spot was called the 'Round House'.

Everyone but this old road layer, who was nicknamed 'Old Motheaten', shook their heads. Old Motheaten said it was all to do with tramps.

He then went on to explain that in Yorkshire as a youngster he remembered a similar place where there was a round house, that had been built at the side of the highway for tramps to shelter in bad weather. I thought that was kind of the local people to think of the tramps.

The next bit I did not see coming and being young and green asked Old Motheaten why they were built round. I had swallowed the bait and now I was ready to be reeled in.

With a grin on his face he said **"IT'S TO STOP THE TRAMPS S**TING IN THE CORNERS!"**

««««««««««««««»»»»»»»»»»»»»»

Lanc and another two lads from the Betteshanger fishing club were fishing about two miles off Deal in a boat they had hired for the day. They hardly had a bite for three hours and were getting a bit despondent. They were on the point of calling it a day, when Lanc said **"Let's row out a hundred yards or so and try out luck there."** They did this and cast their lines out. Would you believe it, the fish started biting straight away. It took them all their time to bait the hooks and drop them back in the water before they had to pull them in again. You name it, cod, whiting, bass, mackerel, they were filling the boat.

"Hold on!" said Lanc after a while **"If we land anymore we won't be able to row the boat back to shore."**

"You're right Lanc" replied one of the other lads **"Let's come here tomorrow and bring some of the other lads."**

"Yeah" said the third lad **"But how are we going to find this spot again?"**

"Well" offered the first lad **"Why not put a cross on the side of the boat?"**

"Give over!" Lanc replied **"WE MIGHT GET A DIFFERENT BOAT TOMORROW!"**

«««««««««««««»»»»»»»»»»»»»

Lanc was suddenly transformed from his usual casual form of dress into a smart suit and waistcoat. On Saturday evenings and Sundays he looked as though he had just stepped out of Burtons the tailors' front window. When one of his friends remarked how smart he looked in his new suit, Lanc replied that the suit and waistcoat had been left to him by his uncle who had committed suicide in the very same suit.

His friend asked Lanc how his uncle had killed himself and Lanc informed him that his uncle had laid on the railway line and had been chopped of at the neck and just above the ankles.

"Wait a minute" said Lanc's friend **"Wouldn't that have ruined the trousers?"**

No" said Lanc **"MY UNCLE HAD THE PRESENCE OF MIND TO ROLL HIS TROUSERS UP!"**

SALOON
J. BRANNAN
84
©

EXPLICIT CONTENT

In what was a physically and sometimes mentally tiring job, 'knock knock' jokes and wordplays were not always enough to make the day go quicker. Here are a few of the ruder anecdotes I picked up from Betteshanger. Some are true, some are fictitious, but none are for the faint hearted!

«««««««««««««»»»»»»»»»»»»»

I remember the early fifties, a retired miner who I shall call Harold to conceal his identity, was in the habit of using the Clarendon Hotel on the Deal Seafront.

Nothing special about that you may say, but the manager of the hotel was what the miners would call posh. But for some reason Harold and the hotel manager seemed to get on very well together and often would be seen chatting and drinking in the bar.

Harold went missing from the Clarendon for about two weeks and when he finally reappeared the manager said **"Harold where have you been? I was getting worried about you."**

"Aye" said Harold **"I've had a bit of rheumatism in the thigh."** He then went on to describe how the doctor had given him a small roller and dish and some liniment to apply to his thigh, and added **"I have to be careful I don't get any on my old John Thomas."** (sexual organ)

The manager felt embarrassed in front of the other customers, but soon recovered his composure and cheekily asked **"Harold do you think that would have any beneficial effect?"**

"I'll tell thee this" said Harold **"IF YOU HAVE NEVER HAD A HARD-ON BEFORE, YOU WILL WITH SOME OF THIS!"**

«««««««««««««»»»»»»»»»»»»»

In the days when coalface teams negotiated their own contracts with the management, one coalface had run into a fault and their money hit rock bottom.

They called a coalface meeting and decided to ask the manager if they could go on a day wage until they got clear of the fault. This was agreed and one collier who came from Derbyshire said **"If the manager gives us nowt it will be a bit of a summat."** (as I have indicated, he did come from Derbyshire).

A miner made a compensation claim against the NCB for losing his testicles in a shot firing accident. When he went before the panel of doctors and NCB legal team, he told them that though it was a thousand to one chance that he was injured, never the less he should get compensation for loss of part of his manhood.

What the compensation board could not understand was why did he not lose his penis at the same time?

The miner did his best to explain how it had happened. According to his story, the heading men had bored the holes and with the help of the deputy had prepared the heading for shot firing.

Everybody had retreated back down the roadway to where the safety net was drawn across the roadway which was the normal safety procedure. While the deputy was connecting the wires to the detonating battery, our miner friend decided to go back farther along the roadway and have a good crap.

He dropped his trousers and squatted down with his back towards the safety net. When the deputy fired the explosives a piece of sandstone no bigger than a golf ball somehow flew past the side of the safety net and headed on down the roadway and took our crapping friends testicles clean off.

The members of the compensation board agreed it was a fluke shot and had no quibble about paying the miner compensation, but one of the panel looked puzzled and said **"From what you are telling us and the position you were in with your back to the explosion and squatting down, why didn't the piece of sandstone take away your penis as well."**

"Well" said the miner **"I WAS THINKING OF MY WIFE'S YOUNGER SISTER AT THE TIME!"** (penis erecti)

««««««««««««»»»»»»»»»»»»

There was one family who came from the North who had about six sons, who all went to work at Betteshanger.

One of the sons got married to a local girl from Deal and after five years into the marriage had four children and one on the way. It was obvious something had to be done, so the lad went along to see Doctor Fraser, an old Scottish doctor who practised in Eastry.

"What am I going to do doctor?" he wailed **"The way things are going the house will be full of kids and I won't be able to feed and clothe them proper."**
"Well" said Doctor Fraser **"It's about time you thought about contraception."**
"What's that?" the young miner asked.

Doctor Fraser tried to explain about condoms, to which the young chap did not seem to grasp, so Doctor Fraser said **"Well then what I suggest is when you are coming to the end of your love making you pull out."**
"I can't do that" said the lad **"I love my wife too much and that is the moment we enjoy best."**
"Aye" said Doctor Fraser **"I LOVE SMOKING MY PIPE BUT I STILL HAVE TO TAKE IT OUT TO SPIT!"**

««««««««««««»»»»»»»»»»»»

This Kent miner's wife had a problem trying to get to sleep at nights.

No matter how she tried to relax and drop off, sleep seemed to elude her. She mentioned it to her husband who told her to go and see the doctor.

The doctor listened to her and said **"It's obvious. You are not getting enough sexual intercourse."**

The Kent miner's wife, not being used to such medical terms asked the doctor **"Where do I get this sexual intercourse doctor?"**
The doctor replied **"From your husband of course!"**

The miner's wife returned home and the Kent miner asked **"What did the doctor say luv?"**
His wife told him **"I've got to have more sexual intercourse and you've got to give it to me."**
"What's sexual intercourse?" asked her husband.
"I've no idea" replied his wife.

"I know one thing" the miner answered **"When the Labour Party came into power in 1945 and created the National Health Service everything is free, and if anything the doctor's got to give you this sexual intercourse, whatever it is."**

The next evening the Kent miner took his wife to see the doctor and when they walked in to see the him said **"Now look here doctor, if anyone has got to give my wife this sexual intercourse it's got to be you."**

The doctor said **"very well"** and asked the miners wife to take all her clothes off and lay on the couch.

The miners wife did this and the doctor took all his clothes off and got on top of the miner's wife and was just about to penetrate her, when the Kent miner said **"Hey doctor, what do you think you are doing?!"**

"I am about to administer sexual intercourse to your wife" replied the doctor.

"Oh, carry on" the Kent miner said **"FOR A MOMENT THERE I THOUGHT YOU WERE GOING TO SHAG HER!"**

«««««««««««««»»»»»»»»»»»»»

There was this young Welsh miner who landed at Deal railway station and all he owned was what he stood up in. Apparently he had to leave the Rhonda Valley very quickly, because he was a bit of a lad for the ladies and a few angry fathers and jealous husbands and boyfriends were likely to do him injury in the nether region.

Lucky for him he managed to get set on at one of the Kent pits and acquired board and lodgings with a young family in Deal. The man of the house also worked at one of the local pits and as fate would have it he was put on another shift from our Welsh Romeo. Before long when the husband set off to work on the day shift, Taffy the cad would slip into bed with the wife, and not just to keep her warm.

The Deal miner and his wife had a young son Johnny who was eight years of age who did not like missing school. One morning Johnny woke up and realised that his mother had not called him, and if he did not make a dash for it he was going to be late.

Johnny dressed as quickly as he could, and grabbed his satchel and rushed off to school without a bite to eat or drink. In spite of his efforts to be on time he was ten minutes late.

He missed assembly and roll call and dashed into class apologising to his lady teacher and sat down at his desk. The first lesson that morning was about the geography of Great Britain.

The teacher looked around the class and her eyes rested on Johnny, who was one of her favourite pupils, and asked **"Johnny, can you tell me where the Welsh Border is?"** pointing to a large map on the wall of Great Britain.

"Yes miss" replied Johnny **"IN BED WITH MY MUM, THAT'S WHY I WAS LATE FOR SCHOOL AND HAD NO BREAKFAST!"**

«««««««««««««»»»»»»»»»»»»»

It's not unusual (apologies to Tom Jones) to see some ex miners with hump backs. This could be because they had worked for years on low coalfaces.

One hump backed ex miner was sat in a pub on Deal seafront on a lovely summer evening, having a quiet drink, and there seemed to be quite a lot of holiday makers about. A rather smart middle-aged lady approached the ex miner and asked if she could buy him a drink.

"Why not?" he thought, and said to the lady **"That's kind of you, I would like a pint of bitter."**

The lady bought him a pint and said **"I always like to come to Deal for my holidays, and love to chat to the local people."**

Both the lady and the hump backed miner chatted for a while, and then the lady, looking a little bit embarrassed, said to the ex miner **"Could I ask you something quite personal?"**

"Of course you can" replied the ex miner **"We are both adults."**

"Is it true that humped back men have big willies?" asked the lady.

"Well I don't know about other humped back men" said the ex miner **"But I am quite happy with what I have got."**
"I don't suppose I could have a look at it?" asked the lady.
"I'll tell you what" replied the ex miner **"Let's sneak out in the back yard where it is quiet and I'll show it to you."**

They did this, and the ex miner exposed his 'thingy'.
"Oh that's a beauty, can I touch it?" asked the lady.
"Oh alright" the ex miner replied **"But don't be too long, someone might come out here and see us."**
"I wont be long" the lady answered, and held it and stroked it.

The inevitable happened, and the lady said **"Oh it's lovely, may I give it a kiss?"**
"No you bloody well cant!" replied the ex miner **"The last woman who kissed it blew down it. THAT'S HOW I GOT THE HUMP ON MY BACK!"**

«««««««««««««»»»»»»»»»»»»»

A word that used to stick in my mind as a young pit worker in the early fifties was 'The Great Divide'. This word was used by Labour Party councillors in Deal to describe what they believed to be the unfair distribution of council money spent on areas of Deal.

It was said at times that council money spending stopped at Manor Road and above there Mill Hill had to rely on the mining welfare to get anything done. Whether this is true or not does not really matter. I am just using this as an excuse for my next story.

There was this miners dog that had a very dubious ancestry to say the least. Although he was a mongrel, he was well looked after and loved by the family that owned him. He was allowed to run free whenever he liked and made the most of it.

One of his favourite outings was to leave Mill Hill and to wander down Manor Road and St Leonards Road and chat through the fences of the gardens of the more select area, to the dogs of the people living there.

One dog in particular was a thoroughbred golden Labrador, who in spite of his noble background looked forward to having a chat with the miner's dog. He probably envied the freedom the miner's dog had and always appreciated the news he got from the miner's dog about life outside his owners garden.

For about a week the Labrador went missing from the garden and when he turned up in the garden again, the miner's dog asked **"Where have you been this week?"**
The Labrador replied **"My owners took me up to Crufts to enter me in the competitions and I did rather well."**

"How's that?" asked the miner's dog.
"Well" said the posh dog **"I got two firsts, two seconds and was highly recommended."**
"I would not mind having a go at that." said the miner's dog.
"I doubt if you would be let anywhere near there" said the Labrador.
"Oh I don't know" replied the miner's dog **"There's a bit of a dog show up at Kingsdown this weekend, I think I will wander up there and see what's what."**

A week later the miners dog made his way down to Manor Road and saw his posh friend through the fence.
"Tell me" said the Labrador **"How did you get on at the Kingsdown dog show?"**
"Great" said the miner's dog **"I HAD TWO FIGHTS, TWO F**KS AND I WAS HIGHLY DELIGHTED!"**

«««««««««««««»»»»»»»»»»»»»

One person who always seemed to radiate sunshine and joy was Jock G, who lived in Betteshanger village.

Jock was involved in an incident with a young girl who lived next door to him when he was a young teenager. He always liked to tell his version of the story and did not, to be honest, need much prompting.

One Saturday afternoon, Jock's mother had gone to Deal to do some shopping, and his father was working down the pit on the afternoon shift. Apparently Jock and this girl from next door who was about Jock's age, had got into a routine of getting into Jock's parents house each Saturday afternoon and with the house to themselves experimented in the art of lovemaking.

Due to a surprise attack by enemy aircraft on Deal, Jock's mother caught an earlier bus than usual back to Betteshanger. On entering by the back door and walking through the kitchen and into the living room, Jock's mother caught them going at it like a pair of rabbits.

Jock's mother immediately broke up the fun and screamed at the girl to get out of her house and whacked Jock around the face and said **"Wait 'til your dad gets home, I am going to tell him to give you a bloody good hiding!"**

Eventually Jock's dad arrived home from work on the afternoon shift and Jock's mum related what had happened and said to her husband **"Give him a bloody good hiding!"**

Jock's father (who was a lot like Jock in his ways) walked into the kitchen and took down a frying pan from the shelf.

His wife screamed **"YOU CAN'T HIT HIM WITH THAT. YOU WILL KILL HIM!**

Jock senior replied **"I am not going to hit him with it I am going to fry him some bacon and eggs."**

"What for?" asked Jock's mother.

"Well" said Jock's dad **"YOU CANT EXPECT A LAD TO F**K ON BREAD AND JAM!"**

««««««««««««««»»»»»»»»»»»»»»

Everybody seems to have a car these days and some have more than one, but in the fifties you were lucky if you had a pushbike, or if you had a motorbike you were really 'Jack the lad'.

Four lads that I knew at that time chipped in together and bought a pre-World War Two motor car. They were able to range a bit further than normal with their own transport and if you believed the tales of their conquests with the fairer sex, it was a wonder they had any energy left to work at the pit during the week.

One story I think we can believe, is the one where they went up to London one Saturday to watch a football match and after they parked the car, which was a lot easier to do in those days than it is now, they went off to watch their football match.

After the match the four decided to visit a jazz club which was the in thing in those days. It was now time for them to start making their way back to the 'sticks' of East Kent and burden their long suffering workmates with fabulous tales of life west of Canterbury. Once they relocated their car they set off for home and in spite of there being less volume of traffic in those days, they soon realised that they were lost.

One of the lads said he could remember coming up the 'Old Kent Road' and said if they stopped and asked someone how to get to the 'Old Kent Road' that would put them in the right direction.

This was agreed on and pulling over to the side of the street they stopped by a lamp post where a hefty lady was dressed in a short skirt, a blouse, fishnet stockings and high heeled shoes, all of which were designed for a woman three sizes smaller.

The lad who was driving looked at her standing there swinging her handbag, with a cigarette dangling from her heavily made up lips and asked her **"Could you tell us how to get to the 'Old Kent Road?"** The lady glared at him from under long false eyelashes and replied **"F**K OFF. YOU DON'T THINK I AM DRESSED LIKE THIS TO DIRECT THE F**KING TRAFFIC DO YOU?!"**

««««««««««««»»»»»»»»»»»»

A bunch of Kent miners decided to have a day trip in Boulogne, on the cross Channel ferries. They disembarked at Boulogne and wandered about the town and for the biggest part of them it was the first time they had ever left the shores of England.

Four of them sat down at a table outside a café and after a lot of sign language and much frustration managed eventually to make it clear to the lady serving them that they would like four cups of tea. The madame brought a tray with four cups of tea, some sugar and a very small jug of milk. By the time the Kent lads had shared the milk out, the tea looked as if it had no milk in it at all.

"I can't drink my tea like this" said one of them.
"Nor me" said another **"I think we should ask the lady for some more milk"**

They signalled the lady to come over, and tried to explain to her that they would like some more milk. As with ordering the tea the language barrier was to cause them a problem again, because the Kent lads did not know the French word for milk.

One of them had an idea and catching the French lady's eye he put his hand on his left nipple and gave it a couple of squeezes. **"Oh"** said the madame and promptly pulled out one of her very ample breasts and squeezed a couple of drops of her own milk into each cup.

"BLOODY HELL!" said the lad who had the idea **"I AM GLAD WE DID NOT WANT SOME MORE HOT WATER!"**

««««««««««««»»»»»»»»»»»»

Two young miners from up North came down to work at Betteshanger in the nineteen thirties.

After getting digs in Deal, and after visiting most places of interest in the local area, they decided to give Dover the once over one Saturday evening. Following a few drinks in a few Dover pubs, and having chatted to the locals, it was chuck out time.

"I think we should be making our way back to Deal" said one to the other.

They made their way to Pencester Road, and found the last bus back to Deal had already left. They then made their way to the railway station, but the same thing had happened there - the last train had gone. There was nothing else they could do but set off walking to Deal.

As they neared Ringwould it started to rain.
"I think we should shelter somewhere" one said to the other.

They looked around, but there did not seem to be anywhere to shelter. One of them noticed a light in one of the houses and said **"Let's knock on the door of that house and ask if we can shelter there until the rain stops."**

They knocked on the door, and an old lady opened it and asked them **"What do you want?!"** One of the miners asked if they could shelter until the rain stopped.

The old lady replied **"I am just going to bed. You can use the armchairs in the living room, but as soon as the rain stops you must go on your way because I am an eighty year old widow, and I have my reputation to think of."**

The two young miners thanked the lady and settled down in the armchairs, and the old lady went upstairs to her bed. After almost an hour and a half later the rain stopped, and the two young miners continued on their journey.

Approximately nine months later, one of the miners received a letter, and after reading it went to see the other miner.

He look at him and said **"I want you to cast your mind back to that time we had to walk back from Dover, and that nice old lady in Ringwould let us shelter from the rain."**

"What about it?" he asked.
"Well when I fell asleep in the armchair, what did you get up to?
The other miner gave a cheeky grin and said **"I went upstairs and gave the old lady a cuddle."**
"You sure it wasn't more than a cuddle, and while you were up there you gave her my...name and address?" said the first one.
"Don't tell me a woman of her age has had a baby?!" said the other young miner.

"No" said the first one **"SHE DIED AND LEFT ME ALL HER MONEY!"**

U.M
ICKET
LINE
J BRANNAN
84
©

THE FINAL YEARS

From a comical perspective I don't want to say too much about the 1984 strike because after a year out on the picket line there was not a lot to be amused about. The bitterness it caused between families, neighbours and friends was in some cases catastrophic and till this day the memories of that time still haunt many ex miners.

There was one incident that I would like to mention that gave us a laugh.

We were on the picket line at Betteshanger pit gates waiting for the strike breakers to come and that morning instead of having the Kent Police there, who we had a kind of rapport with, we had the Metropolitan Police the other side of the barrier.

It was obvious they were looking for trouble. They kept shoving us back from the barrier and threatened us. We had heard from other areas that they, the Metropolitan Police had a method of suddenly snatching someone from the picket line and arresting them.

One of those Met Police, a sergeant was strutting up and down the other side of the barrier as though he was Hitler, or Saddam Hussein.

One of the lads caught his eye and put his left forefinger on his upper lip and did the Nazi salute with his right arm. If looks could kill that lad would be six feet under now. This was a prelude to what was going to happen that morning.

We sighted the strike breakers bus coming along the Deal-Sandwich Road and got ready for a confrontation that was inevitable that day. In the meantime along came this character who we all knew very well with a camera hanging around his neck and a big badge on his lapel with the word 'Press'. This character who was one of us and who I shall refer to as R walked around the other side of the barrier and pretended to take photographs of what was going on. We, of course, made out we did not know him.

The strike breakers bus duly arrived and we pushed forward to show these Met Police that we were not frightened of them that morning. Punches and kicks were dished out by both sides that morning and when the bus finally got through the gates that morning, we fell back to assess the situation, we noticed that the police Sergeant from the Met had got a smack on the nose for his troubles.

With blood pouring down his face he turned to R and said **"Take a photograph of this"** pointing to his face **"And put that in your newspaper."**
R kept a straight face and pointed his camera at the Sergeant and replied **"CERTAINLY. WE WANT TO SEE BOTH SIDES OF THE STORY!"**

Whenever I see R walking around Deal doing his job for the Council I have to have a quiet chuckle to myself.

««««««««««««»»»»»»»»»»»»

For a period of time both Terry and I did the same job at the pit. We were both in charge of a main gate heading, on the coalface, but on opposite shifts. We often changed shifts to help one another with our private and social life. Terry got a lot of mileage out of a story he would tell about the 1984 strike.

He attended a meeting at the Deal Welfare club one day and the Union told everyone there that there would be a big rally in London the following week to keep up the momentum of the strike. The union said that they wanted as many miners there as possible and if they wanted they could take their wives as well. Transport would be put on free.

When Terry got home he asked his wife if she would like to go the rally. She said she would like the opportunity of a day in London and while Terry was at the rally she would like to spend the time browsing around the stores in Oxford Street. This was agreed on and Terry and his wife duly arrived in London on the day of the rally. They agreed a time to meet and went their different ways.

After the rally, Terry had a couple of hours to spare, so he took his time walking to meet his wife in Oxford Street. He was walking up Charing Cross Road when he happened to look in a shop doorway and saw a very attractive young girl standing there. Terry realised that in spite of her good looks and lovely figure she was touting for business, so Terry decided to engage her in conversation.

He complimented her on her appearance in general and told her he was a striking miner and times were hard and if he could afford it he would gladly pay for her services. She said she felt sorry for the miners and hoped they would win.

As a matter of curiosity she asked Terry how much money he had on him. Terry searched his pockets, but all he could muster was five pounds.

The young 'lady' (if you could call her that) looked at Terry's five pounds and said **"Sorry duckey I am a working girl and much as I sympathise with you, I can tell you now you won't get much for five pounds."**

Feeling a bit disappointed Terry left the young lady and carried on to meet his wife at Oxford Street. They met as arranged and set off back to pick up their transport back to Deal. Going back down Charing Cross Road they had to pass the shop doorway where Terry had engaged the young lady in conversation.
She saw Terry with his wife and called out **"I TOLD YOU THAT YOU WOULD NOT GET MUCH FOR FIVE POUNDS!"**

«««««««««««««»»»»»»»»»»»»»

One of my favourite tasks, if you could call it a task, in the final years when the Kent pits were still working, was to take my grandchildren down to the seafront at Deal on a Sunday morning.

If the sea was calm I would skim pebbles with them and see how many times we could make them bounce on the water, plus give them a little treat at the amusement arcade, followed by a walk on Deal pier.

One Sunday morning I was stood on Deal beach with two of my grandchildren when I noticed a lot of anglers on the pier.

What caught my eye most was that a lot of them were wearing NCB donkey jackets. Naturally I assumed that the NCB was holding an angling competition so I decided I would take a stroll along the pier to see if I knew any of them.

Not one of them did I know, but spotting a fellow miner from Betteshanger who was having a stroll the same as I was, I asked him if the anglers were from one of the other pits. Like myself he did not know any of them, so we decided to ask them which pit they worked at.

We asked one of the anglers if he worked at Snowdown or Tilmanstone. He looked at us as though we were off our trolleys and said that neither he nor any of the other anglers worked at any of the Kent pits.

We enquired why he and most of the other anglers were wearing NCB donkey jackets and he said that he and the others had friends and relations who worked at the pits and often put their orders in for donkey jackets, wellies and anything else that was going.

It was no wonder that sometimes when a genuine pit worker went to the stores for a donkey jacket or some other essential equipment, they were told there had been such a demand for certain things that they would have to wait a few weeks for the next delivery!

I mention this because I remember a lad who worked at Betteshanger who was a fully qualified motor mechanic before he decided to work at Betteshanger. The lad in question used his father-in-law's garage to repair his workmates' cars who worked at the pit.

I had my car fixed a few times with this lad and was always glad of this service, but one day he did a job on my car and when I went to pick up my car I could hear him working in the garage, I decided to open the garage door and pay what I owed him.

On entering the garage I found him taking the engine out of a car. This considering he used to be a motor mechanic would not seem out of place, but what he was using to extract the engine was a brand new pull lift. Keeping a straight face I paid him what I owed and departed.

I could understand the odd bit of petty pilfering, but nicking a pull lift, how did they sneak that out of the pit?!

««««««««««««»»»»»»»»»»»»

This Derbyshire lad who worked at one of the Kent pits went to a gala at Dover and was mesmerised with a party of Morris dancers. As he watched them dancing around, banging their sticks together to the beat of a drum, he thought **"I will have to tell my mates about this."**

That night after his wife and he got home from a drink at their local working men's club, his wife said to him **"Another time when you are explaining to your mates and their wives about the Morris dancers, do you mind saying the Morris dancers were dancing to the beat of a drum, not 'They were poncing around to some **** knocking the f**k out of a drum'!"**

««««««««««««»»»»»»»»»»»»

Towards the end of the life of the Kent Coalfield, Snowdown Colliery closed down and those lads who wanted to carry on working in the pits either went to Tilmanstone or Betteshanger.

One lad who came to Betteshanger took a bit of working out. He was always talking about building up his muscles, but when it came to getting stuck in, or doing a bit of work with his mates, it was a popular belief that if he had joined the army it would have been in the Royal Stand Backs.

One day this lad was in a heading with some mates and they were clearing away a heap of rock, so that they could set some rings. What I should have said was his mates were clearing a heap of rock. The lad in question was stood a couple of yards away flexing his muscles and posing as if he was a contestant on Mr Universe.

One of his mates, a little lad who always attacked any job he was given like a Jack Russell Terrier, said to the poser **"What's your f**king game?!"**
The body building enthusiast replied **"I have to do this or my muscles will get soft."**
"I'll tell you how to keep your muscles hard" said the little lad and, picking up the shovel that the muscle man had dropped, said **"TRY USING THIS!"** and threw it at him!

«««««««««««««»»»»»»»»»»»»»

Two Kent miners were travelling up from Deal to London by train.

They both had appointments to see hearing specialists, because they were both as deaf as posts, due to so many years of working in a noisy environment in the mines.

As they grew nearer to Central London they passed a big football stadium. Just after that the train pulled into a station.

One miner turned to the other miner and asked **"Is this Wembley?"** The other miner replied **"No, it's Thursday."**
"SO AM I!" said the first miner **"LET'S GO AND HAVE A DRINK!"**

OUTRODUCTION

In 1989, after sixty years of use, Betteshanger Colliery was closed. But the communities in Deal and the surrounding area live on.

The stories and jokes you have read are what I have remembered over the years since the Kent pits closed. About five years ago I started to write them down, never seriously thinking they would be put into a book. But as they grew I thought maybe, just maybe, some ex miners and members of the public would like to read it.

I hope you have enjoyed reading this book as much as I have writing it. And I hope the memories I have written are pleasant and reminded you of the camaraderie we had.

TIME TO KNOCK OFF AND PUT THE TOOLS ON THE BAR.

View from the top of Mill Hill, Deal, in 2010